Minority Bolshevism

by

Zuriel Redwood

Contents

Part One — Summons

1.1 — Indictment

In the Unites States Court of Public Opinion

We the People of the Unites States

v.

Left Wing Radicals

> a/k/a Progressives
>
> a/k/a Liberals
>
> a/k/a New Left
>
> a/k/a Democratic Socialists
>
> a/k/a Leftists
>
> a/k/a New Bolsheviks

Count One

(18 U.S.C. § 371 — Conspiracy to Defraud the Unites States)

Part Two — Exhibits

2.1 — Exhibit One — AIDS

On June 5, 1981 the U.S. Centers for Disease Control reported that five homosexual men in Los Angeles came down with a rare viral infection. During the next several months many more such cases surfaced. The new disease was named GRID, or Gay-Related Immune Deficiency. By the end of that year 234 people have died of "the gay plague" or "gay cancer" as it was known. In 1982 an additional 853 deaths were reported.

On July 27, 1982 gay community leaders, federal bureaucrats and doctors held a meeting in Washington, DC. They renamed the disease AIDS. Their obvious goal was to remove the troublesome link between the epidemic and homosexuals. They had good reasons to worry. The public slowly learned the scary details and death statistics piled up. The sexual revolution came to an abrupt end. Free love no longer meant happiness, it meant mortal danger. People were anxious and they were getting upset.

A backlash was just around the corner. The Los Angeles County Sheriff Department raided gay bath houses in West Hollywood. Doctors, dentists and hair-dressers refused to serve their homosexual patients and customers. It seemed certain that the gay lifestyle was finished. If the disease didn't get them society would. The short-lived tolerance was over; discrimination and prejudice returned with a vengeance. The future was dark.

It didn't work out that way. Today, more than a million new AIDS cases and more than half million deaths later, the gay lifestyle is back in America. It is celebrated by the media, protected by law and popularized by the culture. Gay rights are all the rage. Same-sex marriage is quickly gaining ground; the military was successfully pressured to accept openly homosexual behavior; and if you are against any of this you are considered a confirmed bigot. Homosexuals are a protected minority. They are a very vocal and very powerful interest group not to be trifled with.

2.2 — Exhibit Two — The Fall of the Soviet Union and Communism

In 1917 — against all odds — the Communist Revolution triumphed in Russia. This surprised even the true believers in Marxism who were convinced that this would happen first in the most developed capitalist countries, such as Germany or England. The newly created Soviet Union survived, despite foreign invasion, civil war, famine and anarchy.

A few years later Stalin took control of Russia. He consolidated his power during the 1930-s, killing and imprisoning countless millions of his countrymen. Stalin's mistakes, however, helped Hitler; and the Second World War almost destroyed the Soviet Union. American and allied help rescued Stalin; and Soviet Communism not only survived but greatly expanded and conquered much of the world. A few short months after Victory Day the USSR turned against the West. The Cold War began.

By the late 1970-s most of the world was convinced that the Soviet Union was invincible. It had the largest army on Earth, including a deadly nuclear arsenal. It was pressing ahead on all continents, chipping away at American power and the capitalist system. It was an undisputed superpower.

Barely a decade later, seemingly out of the blue, the Communist Bloc started to unravel. Russia seemed to have lost the will and the ability to control events. In 1989 the Berlin Wall fell. Two short years later the Soviet Union itself collapsed. It voluntarily ceased to exist. It committed suicide.

At the time these events were widely interpreted as the failure of Communism and the triumph of Capitalism. Free markets have won. Socialism proved to be a dead end. Democracy spread around the globe. The "end of history" was proclaimed. The United States of America was the remaining sole superpower.

Today, just two decades later, everything has changed again. It is widely believed that Capitalism has failed. The sharp downturn of the US housing market and the near collapse of the world-wide financial system convinced many people that free markets are inherently unstable and they cannot be depended on. Large-scale government interventions are demanded. The Federal Reserve bailed out the banking system and the government took control of major auto companies and the health care system.

Left-wing, more-or-less openly socialist governments are on the march pressing the US from all directions. Western Europe is all but lost and Communist China is considered the country of the future. Redistribution of wealth and equalization of income are all the rage. Socialism has returned from the dead, this time in America and the West.

2.3 — Exhibit Three — 9/11 and Islam

On September 11, 2001 Muslim terrorists attacked America. Nineteen radical followers of Islam flew four large airliners into the World Trade Center and the Pentagon killing more than three thousand people. Americans were in shock. The country was effectively shut down for days — like a high school after a shooting spree.

A major crackdown on Muslims followed these events in the US and worldwide. The Koran was scrutinized for clues and reasons for the attacks. Muslims were suspected everywhere. They were searched at airports, their phones were tapped, their mosques infiltrated. The United States soon attacked Afghanistan and then Iraq. Thousands of American soldiers died, many more were gravely injured.

President Bush declared: "Either you are with us, or you are with the terrorists." Most people believed that he was talking to Muslims of America and the world.

Foreign Muslims left America in droves. Many more were turned away at U.S. borders or had their visa applications denied. Islam meant trouble. *The clash of*

10

civilizations between Islam and the West seemed imminent and certain.

Less than eight years later Americans elected a President with a middle name of Hussein, who was raised, at least partially, as a Muslim. US policies have also changed. Islam is no longer the enemy. Muslims are everywhere in America. They are no longer portrayed in films as terrorists, but victims of bigotry, prejudice, racism, and even torture. Often they are shown as innocents victimized by our own military or police. Our government now sides with the Palestinians against Israel. We are trying to be friends with Iran, offering them an open hand. Suddenly, it is cool to be a Muslim in America and decidedly uncivilized to be wary of Islam. Muslim pundits proliferate on television and in the press.

Part Three — Allegations

3.1 — Opening Statement

These three events have several things in common.

All three of them show a complete turnaround in public opinion against overwhelming odds. Unlike most others, these changes of opinion were not caused by sudden, large scale events. No — these changes were slow and deliberate. In fact, they have reversed the effects of just such sudden, large scale events. They were the result of highly concerted and coordinated efforts, massive propaganda.

These changes were also very large. They took several years to achieve and completely turned around very strongly held views of much of the population. Such changes require careful planning and organization, lots of energy, work, patience, and money. Many people had to be involved.

The three events were also very different in some ways, yet very similar in other ways. Considered separately, each one of them can be justified by seemingly reasonable explanations.

In the case of AIDS, gay activists argue that the change in public opinion was the result of basic human compassion. After the initial shock people recognized that gays were the victims of the disease, not the cause of it. After all, not only gays were infected, but all kinds of other people too, even babies.

Left-wing pundits argue that the crash in real estate values really opened the eyes of the American people, who finally could see the shortcomings of the so-called free market. As a result, people realized that capitalism was not good for most of them, and it was only fair to "spread the wealth around".

The same groups also argue that Muslims, similarly to gays, were unfairly blamed for something most of them had nothing to do with. Basic human decency demands to treat all people fairly and equally. Tolerance, especially religious tolerance, after all, is a fundamental American value.

No doubt, many people feel this way. Still, there is something wrong with this picture.

But what, exactly?

For one thing, the odds are against such benign explanations. One of these large scale changes could happen spontaneously. Two would be suspicious. All three of them are highly unlikely. Furthermore, in all three cases, we have come to believe something directly contradicting our own experiences, our very eyes.

While homosexuals really are the main victims of AIDS, they are also the people primarily responsible for spreading the infection. They were the ones who brought it into the country and they are the ones who are still infecting the most people. AIDS still spreads primarily by sexual transmission, especially by anal penetration. There is no way around that fact.

Socialism and Communism have been tried many times over the centuries in many countries and in widely different circumstances. All of these efforts have failed. Existing Socialism does not work and working socialism does not exist. No amount of explanation will change that fact. On the other hand, capitalism with all its faults has worked most of the time.

Muslims did attack America. A clear majority of Muslims of the world consider the US their number one enemy. This is true regardless of country, regardless of education and regardless of social status. While not all Muslims are terrorists, more than enough of them are. Moreover, they themselves tell us that they hate us. Why do we refuse to believe them?

There is a very good explanation for all this. Our case does not depend on the three events cited above. These events serve only to illustrate the underlying machinations and schemes, the well-hidden plan, the conspiracy.

To understand what is really going on we need to go back in time and to examine certain ideas, concepts, events and actions. Interestingly, one of the three events is different from the other two in a very significant way. Which one and why? We will explore that later.

Part Four — The Basics

4.1 — Bolshevism

A brief explanation of the title is in order.

What is the meaning of the word *Bolshevism*? Decades ago this word was more widely used than today. Nowadays, mostly historians use it and it fell out of general circulation.

The concept originates from Russia. It is derived from the Russian word meaning 'majority'. The *Bolsheviks* were a faction of the Russian Marxist party before and during the Russian Revolution of 1917. They were the more radical group within that party, and — supposedly — they were the *majority* within the party. Thus, they chose that name for themselves. Eventually, they became the Communist Party of the Soviet Union. *Bolshevism* became synonymous with Communism, especially Soviet style Communism. This is the ideological interpretation of Bolshevism.

Politically, Bolshevism meant the supremacy of the Communist Party. All other institutions, including the government itself was subservient to the Bolshevik Party. In practice, the Communist Party and the Communist Government overlapped and intertwined.

Since the word means 'majority', it seems to be in conflict with the other word in the title — 'minority'. The full title of this work — *Minority Bolshevism* — actually means: "Minority Majority".

The title was meant to be ironic in more than one way. This should become clear later on.

4.2 — Power

To understand what's going on and how we got here we need to think about the nature of power. We need to understand how power works in different societies and how it works here and now.

Social science — especially as it is taught today — explains power in terms of "class struggle". Not surprisingly, social science today is almost indistinguishable from Marxism. Indeed, the key tenets of social science all originate from left-wing ideology in general, and Marxism in particular. This relationship, however, is covered up, disguised, hidden behind seemingly complex theories.

Social science divides societies into groups — "classes" — according to which groups of society have power. The group or groups with power are designated the "ruling classes". Everyone else is considered oppressed, especially the "working classes", such as industrial workers (the proletariat), agricultural workers (peasants), etc. The middle classes were originally regarded as agents of the ruling classes.

Based on this scenario the concept of "class struggle" was born. The whole idea revolves around the historical necessity of revolution to be waged by the proletariat against the ruling classes, especially against capitalists. This struggle was supposed to usher in a "classless society" along with 'true equality'; first in the form of Socialism, and then Communism. More of those later.

This theory largely ignores one very important fact. Power is not a singular, uniform phenomenon. There are several kinds of power in any society, and they are very different from one another. It is crucial to understand the interplay between different kinds of power if we really want to know how society works, if we really want to understand history and politics.

Economic power is based upon the ownership of assets. Economic power can be further divided according to what type of asset we are talking about. Ownership of money is financial power. Ownership of productive assets (factories, shops, etc.) is capitalist power. Ownership of land or other real estate gives power to the landlord. Ownership of natural resources, oil, mines, forests is yet another kind of power.

The more developed an economy the more kinds of economic power it has.

Political power is a form of social power exercised by governments, other organizations and individuals in order to control people and societies. Political power may be centralized in the hands of a king or dictator, or divided up amongst various groups. Political power can be subdivided into legal power, regulatory power, bureaucratic power, taxing power, police power, and so on.

Military power is the power to make war. Under normal circumstances military power is restricted to states, but this is not always the case. Private armies, pirates, terrorists, guerrillas, insurgents and rebels can all have military power.

Spiritual power is traditionally connected to religions. Popes, priests, ministers, prophets, gurus, preachers, all have spiritual power over their followers. There is also non-religious spiritual power, generally associated with political ideologies, social movements and revolutions. Environmentalism, feminism, animal rights, gay rights, Marxism, nationalism and many others are all ideologies with their own particular brand of spiritual — ideological — power.

There are many other kinds of power, such as individual power, celebrity power, traditions, customs, etc. Professionals often exercise power over their clients, customers or patients. Think of the power of doctors, attorneys, teachers, brokers, mechanics and countless others.

We are mainly concerned with those powers listed above that played major roles in societies throughout history.

Social science today is generally concerned with who has power and who doesn't. While this is important it is only part of the question. The interplay between the various types of power is often more important than the struggle for one particular type of power or for power in general. This is especially true because various groups tend to hold onto their type of power for long periods — even through drastic changes in society.

Social science today looks at history in an overly simplistic way. It teaches that class-based society is immoral and it must be destroyed. It tells us that humanity originally lived in communal groups where everything was owned by the whole society. As private property developed social classes arose. Thus, private property is the source of all evil and it must be abolished. Money, as the essence of private property, is the source of all evil.

Social science distinguishes historical ages according to what type of property the economy was based on and who owned that type of property. According to this view, antiquity was based on the ownership of slaves, feudalism was based on the ownership of land, and capitalism is based on the ownership of industrial and financial capital.

This theory tends to ignore the many other different types of power, treating them as nothing more than mere tools used by the ruling class to oppress the working classes.

In reality, different types of power were in constant struggle with each other throughout history. Each type of power was exercised by a more-or-less well-defined group of society. These groups fought each other through the ages and their fortunes constantly changed. To ignore this as a mere side-show, as an internal squabble within the ruling class is a major mistake, a mistake that reveals a fatal misunderstanding and deliberate misinterpretation of society and history.

Next, we will briefly examine various social structures and historical periods to illustrate and to understand how the interplay of different types of power affects history. After that, we will examine our current predicament. The following paragraphs briefly describe how social science views history.

These generally accepted views are decidedly Marxist in origins; they are over-simplified and thus not really accurate.

Nevertheless, there is no other generally accepted view of history, indicating just how thorough the Marxist takeover of social science has really been.

4.3 — Republics of Antiquity

The ancient republics of Greece and Rome and other city-states were well-developed societies with complex economies. While slavery was paramount, other types of property were also important. For example, during the early republic period a free Roman had to own land in Italy in order to have full citizenship rights, and conversely, he had to be a full citizen in order to be eligible to own land in Italy. Losing either meant the loss of the other.

Some of these ancient republics were democracies. Citizens were free as individuals. They had the right to own property giving them the necessary economic power to secure their independence. Political power belonged to the society of citizens. The state was there to protect the republic and the citizens, not to oppress them. Slaves were considered property — not members of society.

There was constant struggle between various factions for political power. Eventually, political power overwhelmed every republic and subdued political and economic freedom. These republics then fell to a king, a dictator or an emperor.

America's Founding Fathers studied these ancient republics very carefully. These were the only viable free and democratic societies that ever existed. Our Founding Fathers were determined not to make the same mistakes that led to their demise.

4.4 — Feudalism

With the fall of the Roman Empire anarchy engulfed Europe. Centralized political power, taxation, the rule of law, and finally, the economy collapsed. Barbarians invaded the land, and Muslim navies blockaded the Mediterranean. International trade stopped. The Dark Ages arrived.

Bands of soldiers and other fighters occupied tracts of land. Their leaders wielded total power over their territories and their people. They 'owned' the land, exercised military control, and reigned supreme over their subjects. They claimed all economic, military and political power. The only power that could stand up against them was the Catholic Church, which held spiritual power. Since the Church was organized all across Europe, it had to be respected even by warlords. Furthermore, the Church held real spiritual power over all individuals, even the most powerful ones, by controlling the afterlife, by holding the keys to heaven.

Powerful land barons were constantly fighting with each other. Political alliances were made. They transferred some of the political power from individual feuding fiefdoms to the alliance. Leaders of these alliances became princes and eventually kings.

There was constant maneuvering and struggle between the various holders of political, economic, spiritual and military powers. After centuries of abandonment, cities rose once again. Based on their economic power, they acquired political rights and freedoms. Kings, emperors, barons, knights, popes, bishops, merchants, landowners, ship owners, artists, cathedral builders, soldiers, princes, peasants, brigands and mercenaries all fought against each other. Their fortunes constantly changed.

4.5 — Capitalism

Of all the powers described above, economic power is special.

All other powers — political, military and spiritual — operate as person-to-person or as person-to-group relationships. All these powers involve making someone do something, forbidding someone from doing something, taking something form someone, giving something to someone, and so on. All these powers operate on a zero-sum basis. An advantage on one side is matched with a disadvantage on another side. Someone's right is someone else's obligation. The group benefits at the expense of the individual or an individual benefits at the expense of the group or other individuals.

Economic power, on the other hand, has the potential to increase simply by producing things, creating value more and more efficiently. Not recognizing this fact is one of the fatal errors of Marxism and contemporary liberalism. Economic activity produces excess value because the output usually exceeds the input. This is especially true for capitalism.

This is not to say that economic activity is necessarily fair. Often, all or most of the extra output is taken from most of the participants, from the workers and peasants, from the slaves and the serfs. Marxism, however, can only see this outcome out of many possibilities; it can only see one aspect (exploitation) of the free enterprise system.

In capitalism it is far more efficient and practical to divide the excess value produced among all the participants. The owners of assets get their profits — a return on their investment. The workers get their wages — a return for their work. As long as all groups involved get back more than what they contributed the system works well. This is true regardless how fair or unfair the division of the excess value is. The key is the overall growth of the economy which benefits all participants, although not equally.

With the development of more and more efficient production techniques the economy grows faster and faster. Capitalism is nothing more and nothing less than that. It is a move from serfdom to free labor, from subsistence farming to industry, from handicraft to mass production, from shop to factory, from poverty to wealth and the creation of capital. Thus, capitalism is not merely a new method of exploitation. It is a fundamentally different economic system based on creating wealth rather than expropriating it.

Capitalism, of course, is not nice or fair. The interests of capitalists (owners of capital) are not the same as the interests of the workers (owners of labor). But they do share a common interest, the interest in the survival of the capitalist economy, the interest in producing excess value. Denying this common interest is a fatal mistake.

Furthermore, we cannot have an economy — any economy — without economic power. The only question is who exercises that power, who controls production, who controls the economy. As we will see later this is a crucial issue and different solutions to this problem will lead to drastically different outcomes.

Marx refused to recognize any of this. He and his followers were convinced that capitalism was inherently evil and doomed. The early excesses of exploitation convinced Marxists that a deadly confrontation between labor and capital was certain, unavoidable and good. Many of them still believe in Marx's prediction that the great proletarian revolution will soon come; capitalism will be destroyed and replaced by Communism. We see and hear this theory every day, propagated by intellectuals in the Main Stream Media. Usually, it is disguised as social justice, fairness or progress.

Capitalism can only work well in a certain environment. It needs economic freedom which, in turn, requires at least some political freedom. The more economic freedom a country has the more developed its economy is. The more freedom (economic, political, and so on) a country has the richer it is. This is not an accident. Political and economic powers must be separate in a well-functioning capitalist country. They are in constant struggle with each other and this struggle is what this book is all about.

Economic activity, economic success generates economic power. Conversely, economic power is necessary for the economy to function properly. The bigger the economy the more wealth it creates and the more economic power it generates. Large and successful capitalist economies (like the USA) produce immense economic power. Other kinds of power (political, military) are dependent on economic power, but they are also rival opponents to it in a constant power struggle.

There are many other actual and potential arrangements of power. Different cultures in different historic times developed different societies. China, India, Japan and others had different systems. However, they all involve a certain interplay of different kinds of powers.

Economic power is based on ownership. Free enterprise is dependent on property rights. Furthermore, property rights belong to individuals, not groups and certainly not to society as a whole. This does not mean that everything should be private property. It makes sense and it is absolutely necessary to have some things in common, such as roads, parks, rivers, airspace, frequencies, etc. But as a basic rule, productive properties should be owned by individuals.

4.6 — Publicly Held Corporations

This brings up the thorny issue of large corporations. These businesses are commonly owned by groups of people. Some of them have a dominant owner — an individual or a family — who owns enough of the shares to be able to control the entire company. Most large corporations, however, are the common property of many individuals and institutions. Multinational corporations operate in many countries, and their shares are owned by citizens and institutions of different nations.

This common ownership structure presents several problems. The large size and complexity of these corporations require professional management. Management professionals — corporate executives — do not necessarily have the same interests as the shareholders, the actual owners of the company. Yet, much of the actual economic power of the corporation is exercised by these management professionals. Moreover, the exercise of this power is political in nature, as it is based on personal relationships rather than on ownership. Executives are corporate politicians.

Accumulated economic power becomes political power within the corporation. This political power controls the immense economic power of the corporation. Top executives (CEO-s, etc.) often use this economic power in actual politics to influence government decisions. By controlling economic power CEO-s can acquire real political power, sometimes on an international scale. A byproduct of this phenomenon is the constant movement of high ranking management professionals between government and corporate jobs and positions. This is especially prevalent amongst financial professionals. More of them later.

More and more large corporations accumulate substantial political power. They may do this to protect or buttress their economic power or to assure their survival in difficult circumstances. Frequently, however, their very business itself becomes political in nature. Sometimes their economic activity is reduced to a perpetually loss-making enterprise surviving only by political means.

The convergence of political and economic power has both benefits and risks. Properly utilized it can achieve otherwise impossible goals. It can also be used against the interests of the shareholders, or even against the country. Access to political power also enables large corporations to harm small businesses. They are able to manipulate the economics of their field of activity to the detriment of competitors.

Big businesses are a mixed blessing. Their management is not entirely accountable to anyone, neither to the shareholders, nor to the voters. In this respect they are similar to another professional group — lawyers.

Management professionals can be found on both sides of the political divide. Their political affiliations are not always readily understandable, not even to themselves.

4.7 — Free Enterprise — Free Markets

The words *capitalist* and *capitalism* are loaded terms. They were coined by early socialist thinkers, predecessors of Marx and Engels, and they are widely used by their followers, Marxists, Communists, Bolsheviks and the New Left. They are loaded words because they identify a group of people by what they own — namely capital — in a disparaging way. Thus, a *capitalist* by definition is considered an enemy of common people the same way as a feudal landlord or a slaveholder — he is considered an exploiter. Correspondingly, the word *capitalism* also implies a system of exploitation.

This is a one-sided and inaccurate description.

Owning capital is not the same as owning slaves, serfs or even agricultural land. Capital is not a natural resource, it is not limited by nature, and it does not have a finite supply. Moreover, a capitalist may or may not exploit his employees and capitalism is not necessarily an exploitative system.

Free Enterprise is a far more accurate description of the system generally known as capitalism. It suggests that capital and profits are generated by successful enterprises in a free economy.

Another loaded term we often hear is *free markets* or *free market system*. This terminology is often used to obscure and muddle the workings of the free enterprise system. Leftists often refer to more-or-less government controlled, mixed economies as *free market systems,* falsely implying that if the market is free then the economy — the system itself — is free, or at least free enough. Thus, government regulation magically becomes an integral and necessary part of the 'free market system'.

In reality, markets can only be free in a truly free enterprise system. Free enterprise and free markets depend on each other. Limiting one will necessarily limit the other. Free markets, however, are not the same as a free economy. The existence of free markets is necessary but not sufficient for a free enterprise system, for a free economy. Neither free markets nor a free enterprise system can exist without private property rights.

Leftist ideology often misrepresents both free markets and the free enterprise system. They accuse the supporters of free enterprise capitalism of being enemies of laws and rules guaranteeing the fairness of markets and the economy itself. Every time there is a problem they demand more government regulation. By government regulation, however, they mean political interference with economic decisions, not just laws ensuring the smooth and fair functioning of the markets and the economy.

4.8 — Fascism

As we have seen, capitalism requires a certain amount of freedom in order to work properly. This, in turn, demands a balance between political and economic power, or the very least a truce, a sort of non-aggression treaty, a non-violent coexistence and cooperation.

Unfortunately, the necessary balance between economic and political power doesn't always hold. Most often this breakdown happens in less developed countries, or countries with significant social or economic problems, such as wars, riots, famine, revolution, etc.

If such a conflict develops into an open confrontation one side may win and another may lose. If the economic power wins it acquires or subdues the political power. This enables the economic power to achieve almost total control of a country. This is what fascism really means. It is a totalitarian government serving the holders of economic power.

Regrettably, the word fascism has been used, overused and misused to include many different things. Fascism is frequently confused with Nazism for various political and ideological reasons, even though the two are very different systems. The term fascism is commonly used to describe any right-wing political movement or nationalist ideology. Today the word fascist is generally pinned on anything or anyone as an expletive, a swear-word. Leftist activists malign any and all people or views that oppose leftist ideology as fascist.

But real fascism, as defined by its mastermind Mussolini, means the supremacy of economic interests. This is also known as corporatism. Such economic powers often use nationalistic ideologies to further their causes. Examples are Mussolini's Italy, Franco's Spain, and Pinochet's Chile. None of these countries had fully developed capitalist economies. Their economic power was shared with large land-owners and the Catholic Church, and their labor force contained a large proportion of landless peasants.

After the disaster of World War One and the failure of the Weimar Republic, German industrialists tried to set up a fascist state. They thought that Hitler would serve their interests. However, once Hitler grabbed political power he turned on his industrialist mentors. He formed an alliance with the holders of military power (the generals) and instituted National Socialism — Nazism, which is a far cry from fascism. In fact, it is the exact opposite, a variety of Socialism. In Nazi Germany the political and military power dominated everything, including economic power. Hitler soon changed out of his suit into a military uniform.

This is a very important, poorly understood, but crucial distinction. As history shows, fascist states can survive for long periods and they are typically not aggressive towards other countries. Nazism and other similar collectivist systems are far more malignant, dangerous, expansionist, and can collapse far more quickly.

Part Five — Rise of the Left

5.1 — Socialism and Communism

The early decades of capitalism were brutal. This was not necessarily and not entirely the fault of capitalism or the capitalists. Capitalism, after all, grew out of the cracks of inefficient and crumbling medieval economic systems, which were even more brutal. Feudal landlords — the aristocracy — desperately wanted to hang onto their power and they willingly allied with absolute monarchies in order to survive.

Aristocrats (and the nobility in general) were under immense pressure. Huge masses of miserably poor people pressed them from the bottom. Successful and rich new powers pressed them from all sides. More efficient economic powers — bankers based in free cities — lent them huge amounts of money, which needed to be repaid. The discovery of America and colonization of other continents temporarily relieved the pressure on the aristocracy, but only at the cost of relative loss of power.

Capitalism triumphed over feudalism by outgrowing it economically. With the growth of the industrial economy the power of the capitalists also grew. Eventually, they became much richer than the aristocracy which desperately held onto its feudal rights over agriculture and the peasantry. This wasn't always a peaceful process as the French Revolution clearly proved.

Capital does not grow on trees. It had to be created and accumulated. The original accumulation of capital was accelerated — sometimes to the breaking point — by taking as much of the excess value produced as possible from the workers. This was relatively easy as there was no shortage of willing and able workers. They were leaving behind far worse circumstances in their villages. This process was repeated over and over again in different countries as they developed, most recently in China during the last three decades. As a result, each country involved became much richer and more powerful.

Many artists, philosophers, economists and other intellectuals noticed the cruelty of early capitalism. Charles Dickens and others wrote moving novels about the terrible hardships suffered by impoverished workers, especially child laborers. Other thinkers tried to devise social reforms to improve the lives of people at the bottom of society.

One such philosopher was Karl Marx. He distinguished himself from other social reformers mainly by promoting revolution. He advocated the violent overthrow of capitalism and all class-based societies. Most of his work is hard reading, almost incomprehensible gibberish. Most of it is also manifestly wrong. This did not, however, prevent his followers to proclaim him as their patron saint and prophet. After all, he also wrote *The Communist Manifesto*, a relatively brief and straightforward call to arms against capitalism and bourgeois society.

Marx fancied himself as a scientist, as an economist, and as a philosopher. He was convinced that he had discovered the evolution of society, governed by immutable laws. His main work *Das Capital* was published just eight years after Charles Darwin's *On the Origin of Species*.

The notion of immutable laws governing social and economic development has led to countless problems both for Marxists and for their victims, who were sacrificed on the altar of communist ideology also known as "historical materialism" and "scientific socialism". Later on, the obvious imitation of Darwinism by Karl Marx was downplayed by his followers. Indeed, 'social Darwinism' became an unacceptable — politically incorrect — concept. Marxists and other self-proclaimed progressives disowned the idea. They denied any resemblance to Darwinian evolution as purely coincidental, even though Marx himself believed that capitalism follows feudalism and Communism follows capitalism just as certainly as night follows day.

For practical political reasons the definition of Communism had to be reduced to slogans that everyone could understand. This is what Marxism came up with: *"From each according to his abilities and to each according to his needs."* Even to committed communists this goal seemed impossible to achieve any time soon. To solve this problem they devised another stage of development: — socialism. This intermediate stage between capitalism and Communism was defined by another slogan: *"From each according to his abilities and to each according to his contribution."* By the way, the state (government) itself was supposed to eventually "wither away".

Besides aiming to destroy capitalism, Marx had other targets in mind. He and his partner Engels decided that religion and the family also had to be destroyed. The "new man" was not to be burdened with such ancient and oppressive traditions. Clinging to such "false consciousness" was considered reactionary.

These ideas have been reverberating around various societies for more than a century and a half, causing untold suffering and death. Yet, we can still hear these very ideas and these very slogans uttered by more-or-less well-meaning people every day. Unfortunately, many other far more immoral and deceitful people are using these same ideas and same slogans for much more harmful purposes. We will meet them later.

5.2 — Proletariat

Marx identified the proletariat — the industrial working class — in well-developed capitalist societies as the ultimate agent of history, the driving force of the preordained evolution of society. He was convinced that the proletariat would rise up against its oppressors — the capitalists — and stage a revolution. This revolution would utterly destroy capitalism and class-based society once and for all. History — as we have known it — would end; then history — as it should be — would begin. This was to be the communist utopia and it became known as the 'workers' paradise'.

Marx also prescribed the method that history and its agent — the proletariat — should follow. The workers were supposed to destroy capitalism's power structure; first of all the state, the government, and establish a "dictatorship of the proletariat". He envisioned this dictatorship behaving very similarly to the most radical elements of the French Revolution eight decades earlier. The dictatorship of the proletariat was supposed to abolish private property, and thereby end capitalism, exploitation and oppression.

Notably, Marx advocated the use of political power against economic power. The proletariat was supposed to violently take control of political power and use that as a weapon to destroy economic power. The contradictions inherent in this program never bothered Marx or his followers.

Low and behold, Marx's vision came true during his lifetime. In the aftermath of a disastrous war with Germany, the workers of Paris revolted and declared the *Paris Commune* in 1871. The very first communist revolution triumphed and the first communist country — well, at least a city — was established. The dictatorship of the proletariat became a reality. Sort of.

Unfortunately, the Parisian proletariat didn't quite follow the script. Marx was upset with them for organizing elections instead of getting down to business and killing off the entire ruling class of France. He wrote a pamphlet lecturing the *communards* how to properly run their *Commune*.

The heroic but misguided effort was doomed to fail. The *Paris Commune* lasted for only two months. The French army defeated the revolutionaries. Thousands were executed.

Marxists were disappointed again and again. The proletariat refused to follow the role assigned to it by 'history' and social science. Many workers did follow communist leaders but many more did not. Communist parties were afflicted with constant internal strife and petty bickering. When the First World War broke out most workers sided with their countrymen rather than their "class brothers" from enemy nations, as prescribed by Marxism. The anthem of the International Communist Movement - — *The Internationale* — was ignored by the very international proletariat it was designed to inspire. And this was only the beginning of communist tribulations.

Another troubling development was the leadership issue. Invariably, the leaders of the communist movement turned out to be intellectuals, not real workers. When real workers somehow rose up the ranks and acquired power, they sent their own children to universities to study, not to factories to work in. They preached class warfare to others but practiced social climbing for themselves and their offspring.

5.3 — The Kaiser's Gift

As noted earlier, Marx and his followers firmly believed that communist revolutions would first happen in the most developed capitalist countries. Germany and England were their prime targets, although they would have settled for France, too. This premise was very important, as the whole social evolution scenario required society to develop in an orderly manner prescribed by Marx's theories. This was science, after all. Fish had to evolve before mammals. History, however, had other plans.

In 1917 the Great War — World War One — entered its third year. Millions have been killed and much of Europe lay in ruins. Unbeknownst to her people Germany was in dire situation. Despite the fact that the front lines were all in other countries' territories Germany was losing the war. The naval blockade cut off its essential supplies and American intervention changed the odds.

Hearing about the first revolution in Russia — one of Germany's enemies — the German Emperor (Kaiser

Wilhelm II) had a bright idea. He thought he could knock Russia out of the war by fomenting an even bigger revolution. This way he could concentrate on the Western front and possibly win the war after all.

His agents turned up a Russian communist living in exile in neutral Switzerland. The chap's name was Lenin. The Kaiser's agents arranged for a sealed train to take Lenin and his comrades from Switzerland back to mother Russia. They also supplied Lenin with large sums of money in the form of gold coins.

The scheme worked. Lenin and his *Bolshevik* comrades quickly took control of the disorganized revolutionaries in St. Petersburg. A few months later they overthrew the weak provisional government of Russia. This event became known as the Great October Socialist Revolution, even though it happened in November (an omen of prematurity). Within a month Soviet Russia withdrew from the war (as Lenin promised to the Kaiser) and signed a separate peace treaty with Germany, giving up much of Russia's European territory.

Thus, Marxism suddenly became Marxism-Leninism.

All of this was too little and too late, and Germany lost the war anyway. As a bitter irony of history, a mere three decades later, at the end of the Second World War, a victorious Red Army marched into Berlin, raping and pillaging, and cut Germany into two. Even today, the Kaiser's gift keeps on giving.

As a result of World War One four empires collapsed. One of them, Russia, turned into a communist state. Against all odds this newborn monstrosity survived. It withstood foreign invasion, civil war, famine, anarchy and economic collapse. This is how our Exhibit Number Two came to being. A fifth empire — China — soon followed in Russia's footsteps.

5.4 — Disappointment

The shocking victory of the Russian Revolution proved very troublesome, even for Marxists and communists in other countries. They never expected the very backward Russia to become the first communist country. Marx did not predict this and surely he would not have approved of it. Yet, there it was, the newborn child monster. As the years passed Lenin's heir Stalin consolidated his power. And he wasn't satisfied to be the great leader of Russia, either. No — he wanted to take charge of the entire international communist movement. And he did.

Meanwhile, the other European countries slowly recovered from World War One. Communist revolts were crushed everywhere. Marxists were killed, imprisoned, exiled and generally sidelined. They had no choice but to scurry up and submit to Stalin, and beg for his help, if they wanted to survive. Old time communists found themselves outmaneuvered in the Comintern in Moscow. Their very lives depended on Stalin's good will, and Stalin did not have much of that. Many of them didn't make it — they were shot by their Soviet comrades or wasted away in the Gulag.

Marxism-Leninism turned into Stalinism.

Slowly but surely Western Marxism withered away. Its original diversity, social democracy, unionism, etc. gave way to dogmatic Stalinism. After the defeat of communists in the Spanish Civil War and the rise of Hitler in Germany left-wing political parties and their members came under increasing pressure. Many of their members were jailed. Others went underground or chose exile in the Soviet Union.

The center of Marxism shifted to the East.

This was a very important historic development. All left-wing political movements in continental Europe had to surrender to Stalinism and Soviet Russia if they wanted to survive. The only exceptions were the British Labor Party and Franklin Delano Roosevelt's America. Even in these countries Stalin and the Soviet Union had major influence over the political left.

Adding insult to injury, the proletariat — again — utterly failed to follow its role prescribed by Marx. Membership in European communist parties was low and shrinking. To the disappointment of intellectuals, workers seemed to care more for themselves and their families than for revolution. In Germany members of the communist party joined the Nazis in large numbers. Still more disturbing was the situation in the Soviet Union itself.

From the very beginning any rational observer could clearly see that Leninist and Stalinist Communism was a far cry from the ideals of Marx, Engels and other early communists. Despite all the propaganda claims to the contrary, it was all about power, not about building a better future. Any honest communist had to be deeply dismayed. Some were. Only a few of them survived.

5.5 — Antonio Gramsci

One such disappointed communist was Antonio Gramsci, a five-feet tall, hunch-backed, sickly Italian intellectual. He was a life-long communist who eventually became the head of the Italian Communist Party. He spent a year and half in Moscow during the crucial years of the Russian Civil War in 1922-23.

A few years later Mussolini's fascist government threw him in jail. He languished in prison for ten long years until he died there in 1937. He spent his time writing. He left behind 1800 pages of notes, which were smuggled to Soviet Russia after his death. These writings are known as the *Prison Notebooks*.

As fascism and Nazism grew in Europe, especially in Italy and Germany, Gramsci saw that the proletariat could not be depended on to fight the revolution. He also noticed with alarm what he called "Fordism", the American workers' 'treachery' of settling with capitalism for higher wages and a better life.

Eventually, he came to the conclusion that it was necessary to recruit new groups to fight against capitalism. He identified homosexuals, radical feminists, racial minorities and criminals, among others, as potential allies in this fight. He also thought it would be more feasible to wage this war on the field of culture. A "culture war" seemed more winnable than economic struggle or political revolution. He even devised a new strategy against class-based society — instead of direct confrontation and revolution, he advocated a "long march through the institutions". He essentially invented the idea of 'cultural revolution'.

None of this seemed remotely possible at the time. He died in jail without any hope. His rambling manuscript was buried in the Soviet archives, largely forgotten. Everyone was busy with more important things. War drums were beating again in Europe.

5.6 — World War II

The remaining hard core communists outside of Russia were shocked when Stalin signed a treaty with Hitler. They should not have been surprised, since Hitler was an avowed *socialist*, albeit the *national-socialist* variety. Stalin could clearly see that…

As agreed, Nazi Germany and Communist Russia invaded Poland starting World War II in September 1939. With this event the great conflict between left- and right-wing politics moved to the international arena. Hitler, as it turned out, was not very discriminating when he picked his enemies. He attacked both left and right, east and west, north and south.

America, especially after Pearl Harbor, had little choice but to get involved on the side of the Soviet Union and beleaguered Britain. The United States had to choose whom to fight first. President Roosevelt chose to fight Nazi

36

Germany first, even though we were attacked by the Japanese not the Germans. Without American help the Soviet Union and Communism had no chance of survival. Neither did democracy in Europe.

FDR himself was very sympathetic towards the Soviet Union from the outset. Soon after becoming President he recognized the Soviet Union (USSR) and made a deal to settle all cases of Soviet expropriation of American property. He did not bother to send the agreement to the Senate for ratification. Not coincidentally, the Roosevelt Administration was riddled with Soviet spies, even before the war. With American help the Soviet Union developed from a basket case into a political and military superpower within a few short years.

At the end of World War II the Red Army occupied a large part of Europe. In every occupied country communist parties with Soviet help took control within a few years. The countries of Western Europe, especially France and Italy, also had very strong, newly reinvigorated communist parties. Stalin soon turned against his old allies, America and Britain. In turn, American public opinion turned against the Soviet Union and Communism. By this time FDR was dead.

Western communist parties were controlled by Moscow more or less openly. Their leadership was financed by the Soviet Union and received its orders from Stalin. However, not all communists or leftists in the West were Stalinists. All shades of left-wing politics enjoyed a significant revival after the war.

After the Iron Curtain was firmly established political positions solidified. Soviet Communism was on the march world-wide. Western powers prepared for a long siege and chose the strategy of containment. Part of this strategy was to allow left-wing political movements to flourish in the West, especially in Europe.

5.7 — Communism and Bolshevism

All this history begs the question: What is the relationship of Communism and Bolshevism? Are they the same?

Communism is a theory of social philosophy.

Bolshevism is a political strategy designed to grab power.

Bolshevism uses Communism as an ideology.

Communism uses Bolshevism as a strategy.

Both the theory and the ideology of Communism are also known as Marxism.

The relationship of Communism and Bolshevism is analogous to the relationship of Christianity and the Catholic Church (in a different historical and moral context). The essence of Bolshevism is the political party organized to grab power. Bolshevism is actually named after the first such party.

Communism (Marxism) and Bolshevism are historically related. Often, however, this relationship becomes superficial when the group seeking or holding power preaches Communism mostly for practical political or tactical reasons. The best example of this is the Chinese Communist Party after the death of Mao Zedong. Several Third World dictatorships allied with the Soviet Union also chose Bolshevism as a strategy while paying only lip service to Marxism.

5.8 — Useful Idiots — Evil Idiots

During the 74 years following the Russian Revolution many Western leftist intellectuals supported Soviet Bolshevism. They approved and endorsed the revolution, and with it Lenin's red terror, Stalin's purges, the show trials, the Ukrainian famine, the GULAG, the occupation of Eastern

Europe and Afghanistan, Soviet support for terrorism and countless other atrocities.

Some of these Western intellectuals were naïve true-believers, especially during the early years after the revolution. They were dubbed — supposedly by Lenin himself — "useful idiots" to be exploited by Soviet authorities.

After the Soviet Union collapsed the extent of their support became clear. The opening of Soviet Archives proved that many of these Western Leftists were fully aware of the brutal inhumanity of Soviet Bolshevism. They endorsed — some explicitly, most implicitly — the terror inflicted by Lenin, Stalin and their henchmen on everyone within their reach, Russians and foreigners alike.

Many of them were on Soviet payroll for their various services, such as spreading Soviet propaganda, organizing Western Communist Parties and even spying.

After the collapse of Soviet Bolshevism all these people denied any knowledge and any responsibility. They even undertook the effort to whitewash Soviet Bolshevism and blame all its horrors on Stalin alone. In reality, as brutal, savage and bloodthirsty Stalin was, he did exactly what Bolshevik ideology prescribed. Stalin wasn't the only one responsible for murdering millions of people. From the start, Marxism and Bolshevism were inhumane and murderous ideologies that produced Stalin, who carried out the program as written by the theorists.

Despite knowing all this full well, many Western intellectuals supported Lenin, Stalin, and Bolshevism to the bitter end. They were not only "useful idiots", they were also evil idiots.

Part Six — Ascent of the New Left

6.1 — The New Left

During the 1930-s and 1940-s the experiences of the US and Britain were significantly different from those of other Western European countries. The Great Depression caused a significant leftward shift in American politics. FDR Democrats and New Deal socialists were continuously in power from 1932 until 1952. This twenty year period included the entirety of the Second World War. In England the Labor Party was part of Churchill's coalition government during the war, and it was in power for six years afterwards.

After the war the Soviet Union had many agents and sympathizers both inside and outside the American and British governments. Soviet Communism, however, did not present an attractive alternative to the British and American working classes. Both countries had strong home-grown labor movements with leaderships confident in their abilities.

A few American Marxists soon recognized the difficulties of starting a new revolutionary movement. The proletariat seemed to have no appetite for class warfare and could not be counted on. Soviet belligerence, nuclear threats and the Korean War further alienated many Americans. In Britain similar concerns led to similar conclusions.

Die-hard Marxists and other radicals needed a new game plan. Their goal remained the same as before, but somewhat more sketchy. The hope of achieving Communism became more remote, harder to imagine and almost impossible to realize. Life in Stalinist Russia seemed very unattractive. Other Eastern Bloc countries were just as bad. East Germany had to build a wall to keep its people from escaping. No one in his right mind wanted to live like that. Not even communists. *Existing socialism* turned out to be a badly managed prison system and no other kind of socialism existed.

Nevertheless, the Left hung on to the main objective of Marxism. Their goal remained the destruction of capitalism. To achieve this they had to destroy economic power. They also had to destroy the United States of America as an economic, military and political superpower.

US leftists knew that most Americans would not approve of their plans.

The working classes and labor leaders were mainly interested in material advantages, higher wages and benefits. Thus, ideological leadership once again reverted to the intellectuals, just as it was at the very beginning of Marxism. Leftist radicals flocked together around left-wing publications and gathered in left-wing institutions. Freed from Nazi and fascist oppression left-wing politics once again flourished in the West. A large segment of this movement was allied to and controlled by the Soviet Union. The rest set out to remake the movement more or less from scratch.

To do that they had to keep their goals, their strategy and their ideology secret from the very people for whom they planned their revolution. This was all very different from their previous efforts. The movement itself was new. Marxism was reborn as the New Left.

6.2 — New Left Ideology

Having given up on the proletariat, the New Left faced significant problems. Under orthodox Marxism the proletariat was the natural, 'scientifically proven' choice to lead the revolution. It was oppressed and it was vast, representing a large majority of the population in well-developed capitalist countries. By now, however, it became very clear that the working classes were not interested in exchanging their Western lifestyles for the Soviet 'workers' paradise'. Nor were they interested in — or capable of — leading a revolutionary movement.

The leadership issue was easy to solve. Leftist intellectuals felt confident that they could provide the leadership. Deep down they knew that they were always the leaders of the communist movement. They just needed to multiply their numbers. That was harder, but it was doable. But leadership by itself was not enough; they also needed public support. In democratic countries they needed an actual voting majority if they ever hoped to get in power in any peaceful manner — as they were planning to do — by "marching through the institutions", as opposed to fighting on the barricades.

What to do?

Following well established intellectual traditions, they talked and talked and talked. They also read and wrote. They read old Marxist publications and they wrote new ones. Eventually, their efforts paid off. A new ideology started to take shape.

First, they developed new goals. To ensure continuity and legitimacy, and to make good use of nostalgia, they kept the orthodox Marxist vocabulary and the old doctrinal formulas. But they also started to emphasize new issues. They downplayed the idea of Communism; instead, they focused on the destruction of capitalism. They paid less attention to class struggle and more to fighting imperialism. They rarely talked about the dictatorship of the proletariat; instead, they emphasized peace, equality and social justice.

Meanwhile, the Soviet Union was busy rebuilding the communist parties of Europe which were destroyed by the Nazis and fascists. Surviving communist exiles returned from Russia to their native countries. They brought with them ideologies, methods and instructions. Countries occupied by the Red Army quickly turned communist. Now it was the left wing's turn to execute, imprison and exile right-wing elements. They also eliminated members of the previous ruling classes and anybody else they didn't like.

Western countries fared better. Their communist movements were strong but not quite strong enough to grab power. There were some close calls but the lines drawn at the end of the war held.

The Soviet Union didn't neglect Asia either. Stalin sent trunks full of Mexican silver coins to help the Chinese communists. He helped Mao Zedong the same way as Kaiser Wilhelm helped Lenin 30 years earlier. China turned communist in 1949 and turned against the Soviet Union a dozen years later.

Marxism, Leninism and Stalinism gave birth to Maoism. The center of Marxism shifted further to the East.

Meanwhile, in all western countries the New Left was on the rise. Soon the new lefties got the message under control. Now they needed a viable strategy. Meanwhile, they were hiding in plain view, in the shadows of the old Bolsheviks, acting as immature younger followers of the well-established Communist party line.

6.3 — New Left Strategy

At first, the lack of public support seemed like an insurmountable obstacle. It appeared hopeless to try and destroy capitalism without a mass movement. Both old style communists and New Left agitators were looking for solutions. They combed through the forgotten writings of communists who decades earlier fought against overwhelming odds. Eventually, they found what they were looking for: alternative strategies and tactics that were different from the usual mass demonstrations, strikes, uprisings and riots. They didn't discard the old methods either, they just used them more sparingly, and only when the opportunity presented itself. They got smart.

Some of the alternative strategies they came across were the ideas Antonio Gramsci wrote down in his *Prison Notebooks* two decades earlier. The work somehow found its way back from the Soviet archives to the West. Some of his ideas proved to be very useful.

The "long march through the institutions" seemed particularly attractive to New Left intellectuals. This approach promised good results without the usual risks of imprisonment, poverty and general unpleasantness. It needed some work and it was promising only for the long haul, but the New Left had both the time and the patience. So they went to work. Eventually, they figured out how to be both successful at destruction and to enjoy life at the same time.

The old idea of centralized command and control had to go. It didn't work and it made the movement much too vulnerable. It was also unpleasant to submit to a central authority in everything. Rebellion should be fun and — done properly — it could be fun. So pluralism replaced centralism as a basic approach. As long as an activist, an intellectual or a fellow traveler accepted the general direction and goals (namely the destruction of capitalism) he was accepted into the fold.

New groups were needed to replace the proletariat. They didn't entirely give up on the proletariat either, especially the more militant, more organized unionized workers. But the unions sympathetic to their cause were still affiliated with old style communists. The New Left found another Gramsci idea very useful. They decided to turn to other disgruntled groups: racial minorities, homosexuals, radical feminists, criminals and so on. They were also on the lookout for new ideologies. Quite a few of these were developed later on.

They also worked out a new method of recruitment. The "long march through the institutions" gave them the basic framework. They only needed to pick which institutions to attack first. They selected soft targets.

Higher education seemed very promising. It had a built in multiplier effect, especially for the long haul. One radical professor would breed several others within a few years who in turn would produce yet more. Social sciences, journalism and the humanities were especially easy pickings. They attracted sensitive types filled with empathy, ready to take on all manners of social injustice.

The press, radio and television were also natural choices. Each newly minted left-wing journalist, radio or television reporter was worth his weight in gold. They could spread the message far and wide and get paid for it by the enemy, capitalist corporations. Soon they learned how to sell cancer and how to make a profit doing so.

Art was also ripe for the picking. Artists were rebellious by nature; they only needed a little guidance with the message. Writers, painters, actors and musicians were easily recruited for a 'good cause'. So the New Left recruited them. They also cultivated the critics who would decide what was 'good art' to be promoted and what was 'bad art' to be opposed and ridiculed.

The *culture wars* have begun.

For the more hard-core activists there were other opportunities. Long oppressed minorities needed help. These groups had legitimate concerns and sharp resentments. Many women were repressed or abused and most were treated as second-class citizens. They also had immediate and pressing issues requiring solutions, such as divorce, birth control, abortion and so on. The New Left was ready to provide these solutions.

In many parts of America racial minorities, especially blacks, lacked basic civil rights. They were unfairly discriminated against in many fields, employment, education, voting rights and many others. The New Left was ready to help them too.

Homosexuals were living largely undercover and on the periphery of society. When the New Left offered them assistance they eagerly accepted it.

New artistic trends appeared. The most successful was pop music. Rock and roll changed culture once and for all. It also changed society by separating the generations. The lyrics carried simple messages that most young people found very attractive: peace, love, sex, freedom, social justice and rebellion. Social conservatives and large segments of society were alarmed but they didn't know how to react. They often overreacted. Anything they did seemed to make things worse. They no longer spoke the same language as young people did. And there were lots of young people, many more than ever before: the baby boom generation.

New ideas were also explored and developed. Environmentalism turned out to be the most successful. Rebellious youth found a home in the New Left movement too. If you wanted to experiment with drugs, free sex, hobo lifestyle, communal living, new religions, new philosophies or whatever, you were welcomed.

If you were in jail for any reason young lawyers were ready to help you. If you were an alcoholic, a psychopath or just a plain weirdo you could find a support group, a book that was concerned with you, and a young professional eager to help you. Along the way you learned all about social justice, the unfairness of the system and the need to be actively seeking change. You learned who your friends were and more importantly who your enemies were. These turned out to be imperialism, the military, the police, bosses, corporations, capitalism, the establishment, the system and the Unites States of America.

You learned to love the oppressed, the Third World, racial minorities, the environment, animals, radical ideas, modern art and certain political groups. By the time you came out of college you were a New Left activist yourself even if you didn't know it.

In a single generation culture itself has changed. A decade after that it was unrecognizable.

Meanwhile, the international situation also changed. The Soviet Union became a nuclear power and soon after that a superpower. Soviet Communism was advancing all over the world. Anti-colonial national liberation movements materialized all across the Third World. They were financed, counseled and coordinated by the Soviet Union and Red China.

Some of these struggles turned into major wars. American politicians of both parties believed that they had to resist the rising tide of advancing Communism at all costs. Eventually, it all boiled down to the Vietnam War. With this conflict the Left hit the jackpot. The leadership of the country didn't have the guts or the brains required to win the war. Many young people who were sent there to fight didn't want any part of it. The war divided the country very sharply.

It seemed that revolution was about to happen.

6.4 — New Left Activists

The people on the front lines leading these fights were the activists.

Fundamentally, they were no different from the rest of the people, except they took the whole thing more seriously. They were true believers. They volunteered to do things that were not always fun. They spent countless hours in dull meetings. They demonstrated even when it wasn't easy. They got arrested occasionally. Sometimes they were fired from their jobs or evicted from their apartments. Occasionally they were beaten up by the police. Some were imprisoned and a very few of them were actually killed.

Others were smarter. They worked inside the system; they made temporary compromises but violated them as soon as it was advantageous. They got good jobs, got promoted and became prosperous. Eventually, they became indistinguishable from ordinary people who also took compromises. Only their secret hostility and immorality made them different — but that was invisible.

The next step was to make activism a socially accepted occupation. This was not at all unusual. Churches and other religious institutions always had such vocations. The new breed of activists was only slightly different, mostly in their ideological orientation. And, of course, they were paid by the government. The professional activist was born.

Before long, the public developed a seemingly insatiable appetite for 'free' social services. Community colleges turned out social workers in huge numbers. To accommodate this sudden surge, new fields of study were introduced. Each targeted group became the subject of studies by specialized university departments. Ethnic studies proliferated. African American departments were the first; followed by Latino culture, Middle Eastern studies and others. Gender studies, feminism and women's issues also found a place in academia. These studies taught minorities what to think and how to advance these views.

Soon you could major in your favorite social issue; complaint or gripe at any university — or you could major in minority studies. Environmentalism, gay studies, Third World poverty, labor movements, alternative sexuality, modern art, peace, and much else all found home and respect in major universities. Not surprisingly, these newly created fields and their organizations turned out newly minted activists by the thousands. Also not surprisingly, almost all of these newly trained young people subscribed to the same radical left-wing philosophies.

Universities became hotbeds of protest. Students were protesting for civil rights, women's rights, gay rights, social justice of all sorts. They were protesting against the Vietnam War, authority, imperialism, traditions, religion and conformity. Taking drugs became cool; hippies were considered liberated, free sex desirable, resistance necessary. Rebellion with or without a cause was hip.

To be sure, many of these issues were legitimate, at least to some extent. Some of the protests were justified. Much of the movement, however, was overblown and misguided. All of it was manipulated.

On one hand, it was manipulated and financed by the Soviet Union, its undercover agents and supporters. On the other hand, it was manipulated by the godfathers of the New Left, its agents and supporters. The old and new Left also manipulated and exploited each other. They differed in methods and aims but they agreed on the long range goals: ultimately they both wanted to destroy capitalism and its most important symbol and manifestation, the United States of America. Nobody really believed in Communism anymore, except the totally gullible rookies, the naïve foot soldiers of counterculture activism. Some of them actually tried it and lived in communes and kibbutzim for a few months or even a few years. By now, old hippies are receiving Social Security checks and Medicare benefits.

The activists are still fighting the same fights on the front lines.

6.5 — New Left Theorists

The activists were very important but they were not in charge. They were the officers and NCO-s of the movement; not its generals. They were not smart enough.

The origins and traditions of the movement required leaders who were theorists, preferably social scientists. Marxism started out as a science project of a self-proclaimed social scientist. Its main engine was a theory, its method an ideology. To make this theoretical engine work in real life required fuel, actual power, a sufficient social force. Karl Marx tried to graft his theory onto the proletariat, trying to utilize the grievances and resentment of the working classes as fuel.

The New Left had other ideas. They have found a better source of energy.

Regardless of the source of energy, however, the design of the engine was essentially the same. The ultimate goal of the project also remained the same: to destroy economic power and with that to destroy capitalism. Since the essence of the engine was a theory, theorists had to be in charge of the project.

49

In fact, the New Left had a major problem with Soviet Communism. The problem was that Stalin — an uneducated thug, an anti-intellectual — became the supreme leader of the project. To add insult to injury, Stalin systematically eliminated all his intellectual and theoretical betters. Many Leftists preferred Trotsky and others like him to Stalin for this very reason. Stalin left his imprint on the movement; he remade Bolshevism in his own image.

None of this means, however, that Stalin was just an aberration, a dirty stain on an otherwise noble cause and respectable movement. Marxism and Bolshevism necessarily led to Stalinism. From the very beginning Bolshevism was brutal and destructive everywhere, in North Korea, in Eastern Europe, in China, in Vietnam, in Cambodia, in Cuba, everywhere. Many of these Bolshevik powers rose after Stalin was already dead.

After Stalin's death young theorists wanted to reclaim the powers they believed rightfully belonged to them. They could never achieve this goal in the Soviet Union itself. The New Left, however, did manage to slowly take control of the movement in the West.

Mao Zedong in China was a kind of hybrid, like Trotsky, a theorist but also a fighter. He was also decidedly old fashioned, a Stalinist operator.

There were interesting parallels to this phenomenon in history (when a theory or philosophy joined with a social movement and attempted to take control of society). Some of these were: the rise of Christianity, the rise of Islam, the American Revolution, the rise of Nazism, the Reformation, etc. Often these involved the birth of a theory or philosophy, created by a single individual or a very few individuals. The main difference between these and other historical events was that they were planned in advance. The rest of history consists of more or less spontaneous, 'organically grown' events.

6.6 — Social Power

Marx prescribed not only the goals of communist revolution but also the methods to be used to achieve victory. He advocated armed struggle in order to grab political and military power. This victory would lead to the creation of the dictatorship of the proletariat. The movement then would use this unlimited government power to crush all its opponents, destroy economic power, capitalism and class based society.

Marx modeled this path mostly on the French Revolution complete with its *reign of terror*.

By the end of World War II it became clear to the New Left that this strategy was neither feasible nor desirable for several reasons. The leaders of the New Left, theorists as they were, liked to freely theorize. They have learnt from the Soviet experience. They have seen what happens if you give unlimited power to soldiers, to secret police and to bureaucrats. Not only the theorist got killed but the movement itself went off the tracks. They never realized, however, that the tracks themselves were designed wrong.

New Left theorists chose a new, different method. They discarded both armed struggle and dictatorship as viable strategies. Instead, they chose social upheaval to disrupt and damage traditional society. Instead of command and control based dictatorship they chose to exercise social power, the power of status, personal relationships, reputation and prestige. They trusted their own intellectual abilities enough to believe that they could outsmart any and all of their rivals. Gramsci called this *cultural hegemony*. By and large their assumptions proved to be correct.

In some ways this approach was a return to the original practice (if not the original theory) of Marxism, which Antonio Gramsci and others called the "Philosophy of Praxis". Initially, communist activists argued their way into leadership positions within the movement. This was true even during the chaotic days of the Bolshevik Revolution. Lenin was the leading Bolshevik theorist — of course, controlling the Kaiser's money helped too. It wasn't until Stalin grabbed political and administrative power that the smart theorists lost out to the violent thugs and scheming bureaucrats. Interestingly, a similar evolution of power could be observed during the French Revolution and to a lesser degree during the rise of Nazism. There is always conflict between the writers and the fighters, the thinkers and the doers.

The writers of the New Left were determined not to let the fighters take control. This goal was also more appropriate to the objective circumstances they found themselves in. Armed uprising against the newly victorious superpower of America didn't seem practical or even possible.

The theorists of the New Left went to work. They wrote books, articles, dissertations and scientific papers. Most of these writings were obscure and largely incomprehensible for outsiders. They developed their own language, their own vocabulary and reference system.

What appeared as meaningless gibberish to the uninitiated were actually coded messages to movement insiders. Eventually, most of the first generation of theorists attained tenured professorships at leading universities and in research institutions. They proceeded to teach their followers their theories of philosophy and social science along with their language and all the other knowledge necessary to understand their messages.

6.7 — New Left Intellectuals

The people who learned from the master theorists — the founders of the New Left — became the new intellectuals.

Most of them were professional activists disguised as ordinary professionals. They were professors and teachers, journalists and writers, actors and directors, musicians and comedians, lawyers and bureaucrats, social workers and government agents, union and community organizers, and so on.

They all had their respective professional associations or unions. These organizations looked after the interests of their members, and more importantly, they also made sure that the prevailing theories were followed. These various organized social groups were not all the same. There were significant differences in their degree of support for leftist causes and policies. Some professions and some organizations resisted leftist pressure a lot longer than others. Eventually, however, they all caved in.

Today, practically all intellectuals and all professionals subscribe to leftist philosophies and policies. Some more than others, but they all accept the basic principles of the New Left. Their organizations are even more uniformly left-wing. This is because followers of left-wing ideology have a majority in all of these institutions. Individual opponents are simply outvoted within each group.

There are, of course, some intellectuals who are not part of the Left. They are, however, few and far between. They are also constantly ostracized by their peers and they are under constant pressure from the Left. Their careers suffer. Only a very few of them could overcome these obstacles. Many cultural fields seem to be entirely devoid of them.

6.8 — New Left Methods

New Left theorists had to develop new methods to control the movement. They needed a system to compel people to follow instructions that often seemed vague, incomprehensible, senseless, pointless and objectionable. This was not an easy task; especially since they didn't have the power to force people to comply.

The system they developed is quite ingenious. It is a complex hierarchical system of rules, dogmas and taboos. All individual elements of this system are simple, straightforward and seemingly obvious assertions and principles. Common sense and basic decency seem to require full acceptance of them. Often complex issues are reduced to simple but attractive slogans. Over the years many of these commandments were further reduced to simple expressions, sometimes to a single word with a special meaning.

Here are just a few examples:

Capitalist exploitation.

Private property is theft.

Environmental degradation.

International cooperation.

International community.

Government oppression.

Arms control.

Gender equality.

Gay community.

Diplomatic solution.

Solar power.

Homophobia.

Living wage.

Endangered species.

Recycling.

Homeless.

Organic.

Diversity.

Civilian casualties.

Nuclear free.

Sanctuary city.

Green jobs.

Equal opportunity.

Progressive movement.

Progressive taxation.

Racial discrimination.

Community participation.

Community organizing.

Public responsibility.

Stakeholders.

Affirmative action.

Racial profiling.

Voting rights.

Sexual harassment.

Gay rights.

Profit motive.

Gay marriage.

Gender gap.

Sexual orientation.

Social justice.

Civil rights.

Non-discrimination.

Imperialism.

Equal pay.

Voter registration.

Democracy in action.

Undocumented worker.

Gun lobby.

Peace process.

Developing nations.

Pollution.

Government regulation.

Partial birth abortion.

Religion of peace.

Hate crime.

Sensitivity training.

Sexism.

L.G.B.T.

Muslim community.

At first sight most of these expressions seem to simply describe everyday concerns of ordinary people. But this is not true. They all carry a huge baggage. They all come with very specific requirements of how to think about them. They all represent well defined leftist values, political positions. There is only one accepted way to think about them. Only one.

Once a concept was created and refined the entire left-wing movement set out to securely implant it in the public consciousness. Concepts considered good were reinforced by countless stories, books, movies, songs, articles and so on. They were explained, illustrated, proven, promoted, advanced, advocated and supported. All their inherent complexities and contradictions were swept away. At the end they became unquestionable dogmas.

Similarly, concepts considered undesirable were rejected and vilified by the same stories, books, movies, songs and articles. They were declared evil, proven wrong, denounced, objected to, criticized and condemned. All their complexities were ignored. At the end they became forbidden thoughts, unmentionable taboos.

This is, for example, how the fight against slavery and racial segregation became a movement against racial discrimination, eventually leading to the condemnation of discrimination in general. It does not matter anymore that the concept of discrimination by itself is neither positive nor negative. The very idea of discrimination is considered evil in any context even if this makes no sense at all. We no longer dare to discriminate even between friends and enemies.

For example, anyone who is against illegal immigration is immediately denounced as anti-immigrant by deliberately ignoring the differences between legal and illegal immigration.

If you dare to question the wisdom of gay marriage you are condemned as a bigot or an idiot or both.

Of course, other social philosophies also have their ideology along with a favored vocabulary. The difference is that none of these competing ideological systems are enforced all across society. Today, left-wing ideology totally dominates the political and social discourse. It is a totalitarian ideology.

New Left values became universal. These values are accepted by lots of people, and they are imposed on all.

These concepts are now deeply embedded in our value system. As long as one follows the rules (almost entirely set by the Left) one is safe. Any deviation, however, has immediate and harsh consequences. It is better not to even think about these things and it is certainly unwise to question their validity. So most people don't think about them. They just repeat them endlessly and automatically, further reinforcing their power.

And this is not all.

6.9 — Political Correctness

The most ingenious component of this system is the grid of forbidden conclusions. Hidden behind the complex web of dogmas and taboos there are forbidden subjects, forbidden thoughts and forbidden conclusions. Any question that may lead to a forbidden conclusion must not be asked. Any idea that may lead to a forbidden conclusion must not be thought of.

For example: the entire gay rights movement is based on the presumption that gay people are born homosexual. Being gay is not a choice the dogma insists. The logic based upon this presumption suggests that any argument against any rights gay people claim is inherently unfair. Anyone who opposes the idea of gays in the military is immediately accused of hating gay people. Not just that, but he hates gays for what they are. How unfair is that? They are, what they are, they can't help it. They should have the same exact rights as everyone else. Gay rights, therefore, are natural and beneficial to society according to leftist dogma.

But is the underlying presumption true? Clearly, some gays were born homosexual. But all of them? Is it possible to become homosexual some other way? Perhaps, by being segregated from the opposite sex for long periods? Or just by simply exploring intimacy with someone of the same sex? Can a high school boy become gay by accepting oral sex from another male? Was this possibility properly researched? What are the implications to education policies if this turns out to be a common occurrence? Is the spreading of homosexuality a positive development? Is this irrelevant, bothering only prejudiced conservatives?

These and many other questions are never asked and cannot be asked today. Many of these issues have far reaching consequences. In fact, if we dig down deep enough, under most of these dogmas and taboos we can find a hidden presumption that was never properly examined — much less proven — yet, it can never be questioned.

This is the essence of political correctness.

It is not just an annoying fad. Political correctness is a devastating weapon that attacks our very ability to think clearly about the most important issues of the day. It prevents us from making the right decisions. It defeats us before the battle even began. How can we argue if certain conclusions are forbidden in advance? As Bismarck remarked in another context: "One cannot play chess if sixteen of the 64 squares are forbidden from the beginning."

The New Left cannot take full credit for the invention of this insidious weapon. Totalitarian ideologies always practiced some version of political correctness. The divine rights of kings, papal infallibility, the Holy Trinity, the Virgin Birth, dialectical materialism, the Aryan race, and many other dogmas were considered unquestionable truths. Some of them still are. Islam has a very elaborate system of thought control. Violations of these dogmas and taboos were often punished by death and torture.

Soviet Bolshevism gave birth to political correctness as we know it today. Back then the term referred to actions or statements that were not illegal but were against the approved standards of the political leadership. Being politically incorrect was not necessarily punished legally, but it had political consequences. Since political power ruled everything these ramifications were quite serious.

Compared to these standards the New Left is more lenient but not any less dogmatic.

They are politically more correct, if you will...

6.10 — Multiculturalism

Multiculturalism is a crucial aspect of political correctness. It is an essential ingredient because it provides and secures a vital strategic advantage for the New Left. It is a precision weapon, a political smart-bomb used for a particular purpose.

Multiculturalism is marketed as a natural and benign extension of equality. Equality itself, however, is willfully and deceitfully misinterpreted as we will see later. Aside from that, multiculturalism is a far more devious tactic.

The logic is deceptively simple: People are equal in all respects. They should not be held responsible for what they are and they should not be discriminated against because of their differences. If all people are equal, their cultures must also be equal. We should not be prejudiced against people, groups or nations just because they have different habits, customs, traditions, languages, religions, rituals, laws, behaviors, values, etc. We should even go one step further and celebrate our differences and place a high value on diversity. We can all appreciate the variety of food offered by different national cuisines, so why not accept other cultural differences?

What is wrong with this proposition?

Quite a lot, actually.

First of all, food, music and art are not normative values. One can eat Chinese food one day and hamburgers the next without any problems. The same is not true for many other values, customs, traditions, religions, rituals, laws and rules of behavior. Furthermore, the concept of multiculturalism undermines the very essence of America, the idea of the melting pot, the motto of the nation as stated on the Great Seal of the United States: "E Pluribus Unum" — "Out of many, one".

Multiculturalism is a fairly recent phenomenon. Not surprisingly, it gained acceptance during the ascent of the New Left. This is not a coincidence. As we have seen, the old left was unable to convince the majority of western societies to support its causes. After this failure the New Left changed strategy and focused on organizing minorities. Therefore, it is in the interest of the New Left to increase the number of people who are members of various minorities and decrease the number of people who belong to the majority.

That is the whole idea — the strategy of *Minority Bolshevism* — to make a majority out of an alliance of minorities. Multiculturalism is an ideological weapon in this fight designed to fragment society. It urges people not to assimilate, to retain their separate identities, their minority status. Multiculturalism even promotes regression and segregation. The New Left encourages members of already assimilated ethnic minorities (and others) to "return to their roots". This romantic notion is actually a clever plot to break up the majority into many minorities. These efforts — identity politics — coupled with current immigration policies (since 1965), are very beneficial to the New Left, but they are detrimental to America. Similar problems resulted from similar policies all over Western Civilization.

Multiculturalism is widely promoted by the New Left. Its basic beliefs and tenets are constantly popularized by the media, by movies, TV commercials, product advertisements, and the culture in general. Multicultural values are fiercely defended by political correctness. These values are studied and taught in schools, colleges and universities under the subjects of "cultural studies", "ethnic studies", "gender studies" and the like.

Originally, multiculturalism was a means to an end. The proclaimed end was a more equal, a more just, a more harmonious society. The hidden goal was to advance the interests of the New Left. The means were the efforts to promote exclusive and antagonistic rival cultures at the expense of the majority one.

Soon, multiculturalism became an end in itself. Diversity was anointed as one of the highest values to strive for. Universities, large corporations and other institutions aspire to increase diversity for its own sake, often ignoring other important values, such as basic fairness and common sense. Rigid quota systems were instituted to ensure maximum diversity possible. Multiculturalism became the *prime directive of the United Federation of Minority Bolshevism*. Today, we worship diversity and we sacrifice our future on its altar. The New Left benefits. America and the West pay the bills.

Part Seven — Minority Bolshevism

7.1 — Building Coalitions

With the emergence of the theorists, the activists, and the intellectuals the required social force was established. The leaders of the New Left movement — the vanguard — were ready. The rapid increase of their numbers was also assured. These groups of people essentially served the same purpose as the Communist Party did before them. Their function was to lead the movement. They were the new and improved Bolsheviks.

The New Left had a well-organized movement with competent leadership and a popular and workable program.

But this was still not enough.

A movement needs followers not just leaders. It needs foot soldiers not just generals and officers. Having chosen a more-or-less non-violent path to power they needed more votes. The "long march through the institutions" provided the New Left with a blueprint to gain significant power over many aspects of society and culture. The New Left was in the position to achieve ideological power, but this by itself was not enough to grab political power. To acquire political power they had to win elections. They needed public support.

What to do?

A few bright theorists could clearly see the path ahead. They understood the nature of power. They recognized and understood Marx's mistake.

7.2 — The selfless and the selfish

Marx fell into his own trap. He wanted to be the greatest social scientist of all times, the Darwin of social science. He mixed the philosophy of Hegel, the economics of Ricardo, the social activism of French revolutionaries and British socialists into a pseudo-scientific hodgepodge. He believed his own theory. His followers dutifully marched into the same trap.

Throughout their history Marxists were often confronted with a curious observation. They frequently complained about the apparent failure of the working classes to understand their role in history. After the total collapse of Communism they kept repeating their main excuse: 'the theory was correct, the people failed'. Diehard Marxists still believe that the ungrateful people failed the theory, not the other way around.

New Left theorists eventually recognized the error. They finally understood that different people are motivated by different things. They realized that if they wanted to win they had to offer a whole range of reasons and promises to motivate people with different interests, causes and goals. They couldn't expect the people to conform to the ideology, so they adjusted the ideology to please the people. They modified their teachings to accommodate the fickle emotions and limited intelligence of their target audiences.

They embarked on the greatest marketing effort of modern times.

Motivation can be internal or external. Internal motivation is primarily psychological (subjective). External motivation is mostly real (objective), usually economic or otherwise interest-driven. Selfless people can be influenced ideologically or emotionally. Selfish people can be manipulated with economic and other incentives. The great majority of people belong to the selfish category. The majority of Leftists belong into the selfless category. This gap had to be bridged if the New Left were to succeed.

Most people are influenced by a complex set of overlapping and sometimes contradictory motivations. Yet, most people have a primary motivational mechanism governing both their psychological and social attitudes. Indeed, the lack of such primary internal guidance often indicates antisocial or even psychopathic tendencies.

7.3 — Ideologically Motivated Groups

Idealism is both a philosophical theory and a psychological frame of mind; a way of thinking, a point of view, an attitude.

Idealists believe in higher values, personal growth, social justice, helping others, meaningful relationships and a better future. Their primary emotion is empathy. They feel other people's pain, they long for love and understanding, they want to contribute to society. They yearn for peace and cooperation. They are attracted to mysticism, to theories, to spirituality. They are selfless. They want to help everyone. Some of them also crave power. Lots of power.

The core of the New Left is made up of idealistic people. In fact, the New Left cornered the market in idealistic people, with one exception: traditional religions.

Traditional religions, especially monotheistic religions, acquired monopoly power over ideology, idealism and idealists. Christianity started out much like the New Left, as a struggle for higher values and a better world. Judaism and Islam were much more pragmatic from the start. After a few centuries Christianity came around too. Traditions, rituals, conservatism and self-interest overcame ideology and idealism. Traditional religions absorbed and assimilated idealism. They provided a home for idealistic people as long as they didn't interfere with the power of the leaders. This uneasy relationship lasted for many centuries to this day.

Meanwhile, economic and social upheavals and revolutionary movements destroyed medieval societies. Idealistic people started to look for alternatives outside traditional religions. Collectivist philosophies, including Marxism and Nazism, attracted many of them. Finally, the failure of Soviet Communism drove idealistic young people into the arms of the New Left.

New Left theorists developed new alternatives that were more attractive to young people than traditional religions or orthodox Marxism. Instead of forcing them into a comprehensive but rigid belief system the New Left gave them choices. They could pick any cause their heart desired. They didn't have to follow tiresome rules; they didn't have to perform tedious rituals. They didn't even have to make material or monetary contributions. There was no evident authoritarian theology.

All beliefs, all ideologies, all groups were accepted into the fold, no matter how extreme.

There were only two requirements. The first requirement was that all individual members and all groups had to accept all other groups, all other beliefs, all other agendas, no matter how extreme. Most of the time this was not a problem. These beliefs and agendas were usually not in conflict with one other. In the rare cases when such conflicts developed the 'higher good' had to prevail. This was the second requirement. All beliefs and agendas had to submit to the ultimate goal: the destruction of economic power, capitalism and American Imperialism. Even the *prime directive* itself, multiculturalism, had to yield to this magnificent purpose.

Numerous groups joined the New Left project pretty much as Antonio Gramsci prophesized a generation before. Every one of them endorsed the ultimate goals and every one of them accepted every other group and belief, no matter how extreme.

The natural outcome of this arrangement was that each group came under the leadership of its most radical members with the most extreme views. This was partly the result of inertia. People with the most extreme views and agendas tended to be also the most outspoken and the most active. They participated in more meetings and demonstrations and they worked harder. It was also a function of group dynamics. The more extreme a person was the more attention he received. Extremism was interesting. Radicalism was attractive. Revolutionary was chic (cool in today's terminology). Che Guevara rocked. He still rocks.

Not all ideologically motivated people are idealists. In fact, the majority of them are attracted to a single cause. Many of these single cause activists are members of minorities. All of these minorities rally around their organizing principle, their common cause and essence: race, gender, sexual orientation, environmentalism, animal rights, anti-imperialism, etc. While their cause often corresponds to their own self-interests, they are usually not involved for personal advantage. The ones who are involved for selfish reasons invariably take advantage of the rest.

7.4 — Racial Minorities

Racial and ethnic conflict always played a major part in American history. Native Americans versus colonists, Irish versus English, Latinos versus Anglos: every generation witnessed a dominant confrontation between different ethnic groups.

None of them came close to the centuries long hostility between blacks and whites, African-American slaves and European-American slaveholders. The pinnacle of the conflict was the Civil War which claimed more lives than any other war in American history. Yet, a century and a half later the conflict is far from over.

Centuries of slavery followed by decades of oppression, persecution, segregation and discrimination made blacks distrustful of all white people. They banded together under the leadership of black intellectuals, preachers, business and community leaders. They voted largely Republican, the party of Abraham Lincoln.

To escape continued racism and poverty millions of blacks migrated from rural Southern states to Northern cities during the early decades of the 20th Century. Farmhands became industrial workers and miners in huge numbers. This was a significant change for the black migrants themselves but also for the country as a whole. These changes had far-reaching social and political consequences. Enter the labor unions.

7.5 — Labor Unions

Originally, the American labor movement was organized by skilled workers along trade or craft lines. Craft unionism was a direct descendant of medieval guilds. They protected their trades against outsiders and presented a united front towards employers and customers. Usually, they did not admit minorities. Craft unions were primarily based on economic power. They operated like cartels; they controlled the supply of skilled labor, much like OPEC controls the supply of oil.

Rapid industrial development changed the economic landscape. The birth of mass production and the assembly line made many trades and occupations irrelevant. Skilled labor was steadily losing power and this power did not accumulate to benefit unskilled labor. It mostly benefitted employers, capitalists. To counter this slide industrial workers and miners started to organize. They had no territory to defend and they had nothing to lose. Their strength was in their numbers. To increase their numbers and their power they admitted large numbers of black workers in the swelling industrial cities. They tried to regain their lost power by cornering — monopolizing — the entire labor market, skilled and unskilled. This was an uphill struggle. Labor's only chance was to acquire political power to make up for its lost economic power.

A conflict was brewing within the union movement. Industrial unions challenged the dominance of craft unions. Socialist and communist inspired unions also rose in importance. Various federations of unions were established; merged with each other then separated again. One of the most important was the CIO (Congress of Industrial Organizations). The CIO accepted African Americans from its inception.

The stock market collapsed in October 1929. The Great Crash devastated American Capitalism. The financial system lay in ruins. Soon the real economy broke down too. Unemployment skyrocketed. Nothing seemed to work. Politicians appeared helpless.

After twelve years of Republican governments the country was ready for *change*. The *change* came when Franklin D. Roosevelt was elected President in 1932. Among others, he was supported by labor unions, including the CIO. For the first time since the Civil War millions of blacks voted for a Democrat. Seven decades had to pass for this to happen.

FDR's New Deal programs pushed back capitalism and advanced Socialism. He promoted political power at the expense of economic power. FDR did not let the crisis go to waste; he increased the power of government in order to reduce the influence of business.

7.6 — African Americans

FDR built the New Deal Coalition which held power for two generations. African Americans were staunch Roosevelt supporters and more than seven decades later they remain some of the most reliable voters for the Democratic Party.

They do so even though the Democratic Party proved to be a mixed blessing for ordinary blacks. Southern whites were a very powerful voting bloc within the Democratic Party until 1964 and they were not exactly friendly to African Americans. The Roosevelt Administration itself discriminated against blacks, especially in housing. The notorious neighborhood redlining and mortgage discrimination codified by the National Housing Act of 1934 was largely responsible for the creation of inner city black ghettos.

The Democratic Party interfaced with its black supporters through African American community leaders. Hand-picked black union organizers, professors and activists trusted by the black community rose in power within the

Democratic Party. Some of them became advisors to Roosevelt. Known as the *Black Cabinet*, members of the *Federal Council of Negro Affairs* became prominent members of the New Deal establishment.

By his Executive Order 10925 President Kennedy established Affirmative Action to remedy historical racial bias. Later on, this concept expanded to cover nearly all minorities and spread through the entire economy and all social institutions and structures.

As the New Left gradually took control of the Democratic Party they inherited its various constituents, including African Americans. The transition was difficult. New Left tactics and ideology preferred more extreme elements. At the same time the Civil Rights Movement was moving ahead full speed. Martin Luther King was assassinated. The Black Panther movement became a prominent political force. Riots flared up in big American cities. Unseen from the outside an internal struggle raged within the black community. New Left radicals fought against the old black establishment. Eventually, the New Left won.

The New Left also proved to be a mixed blessing for ordinary African Americans. Governed by extremist views it wreaked havoc in black communities. The destruction of the family and religion (along with private property) was always a major goal of leftist ideology. Engels, co-author of the *Communist Manifesto*, fired the first shot with his 1884 treatise entitled *The Origin of the Family, Private Property and the State*. A hundred years later his wish to destroy the bourgeois family became reality in African American communities. The New Left accomplished it in a single generation.

As a result, generations of black kids were born outside of wedlock and raised without a father. They were 'educated' in inner city schools often by teachers whose only qualification was their membership in the teachers' union and their willingness to tow the New Left party line. Unemployment, drug addiction and crime became a normal part of black existence in the inner cities. Huge numbers of young black men are in prison. Policies of the New Left were a direct cause of these pathologies.

Yet, African American activists and community organizers largely support the very policies and the very politicians responsible for these outrages. They promote welfare policies that are destroying the black family, they support education policies that fail to teach black children and they support politicians who use blacks as cannon fodder in their war against capitalism and America. They are no better than the native collaborators of colonial powers. They also benefit economically from their treason.

The lucky African Americans who could achieve middle class status escaped the ghettos. They largely cut themselves off from the rest of the black community. Yet, most of them kept the resentment against white society and they remained loyal to the Democratic Party. They were not offered any viable alternatives.

The New Left interfaced with its black supporters through a new generation of African American community leaders. Many of these activists were dedicated true believers in the cause, waging a seemingly hopeless fight to provide a better life for their people. Others were more ruthless and calculating. They took advantage of the plight of fellow blacks to advance their own agendas. Some advanced their political careers, others operated a shakedown racket. A few did both simultaneously.

Pressured by these forces the American government spent untold billions of dollars to improve the lives of African Americans over several decades. In material terms their lives did improve. Their living standards rose. They had more money. A significant black middle class developed. But the well-being of ordinary blacks remained an elusive goal. Black communities deteriorated further and further. Many of them became virtually unlivable.

How could this be?

Neither the old nor the New Left really cared for African Americans. With the exception of a few die-hard true believers they gave up on blacks long ago. They view African Americans as a strategic asset, as a reliable voting bloc, as a political weapon to wield against Republicans, especially Southern Republicans, and against capitalism.

Unfortunately, the Right and the Republican Party did not care for African Americans either. By and large they wrote off blacks as a lost cause. Most Republican efforts designed to attract black voter appeared half-hearted, as a mere afterthought.

When the interests of blacks conflict with the interests of others within the New Left coalition blacks generally lose out. They lost out to teachers' unions, prison guard unions, and large financial institutions, among others. It is a well-known fact that the Democratic Party takes African Americans for granted. They have a vested interest in the status quo, in the continued disenfranchisement and discontent of blacks. Blacks are also sold out by other blacks to white interests as they were for centuries.

There is no visible alternative. We have to provide one. Change is possible, but it would require a change of heart by a significant portion of African American community leadership or the emergence of a new leadership.

7.7 — Latinos

Latinos are the fastest growing racial/ethnic minority in America. They already bypassed blacks as the largest minority. Blacks and Hispanics together comprise almost a third of the US population.

Despite some similarities Latinos represent fundamentally different problems than blacks. These problems are more troublesome and more difficult to solve.

African Americans are Americans. They speak English. They have no other allegiances in any meaningful sense. Despite all the problems and conflicts African Americans' closest relationship is with white America. This is not the case with many Latinos.

Many Latinos are intimately connected to other countries, especially Mexico. A significant percentage of Hispanics feel a strong kinship to foreign countries and their citizens. Even after living in America for several generations these connections can remain very strong. Coupled with legal and illegal immigration these issues present a major problem. Close proximity and the long common border further aggravate an already difficult situation. Radical Latino activists exploit these intrinsic human emotions.

Speaking Spanish also presents an economic and — more importantly — a cultural barrier. A lot of meaning is lost in translation.

Clearly, uncontrolled immigration would devastate America in the long run. If Latinos became the majority, the Unites States as we know it would cease to exist. Everyone knows this but it is politically incorrect to voice such concerns. Yet, this is a simple fact, not only a value judgment. America with a Latino majority would be a Latin American country by definition. Mentioning this issue, however, is considered racist, as is to worry about Hispanic immigration, legal or illegal.

Such a change seems to be far in the future. In reality, by 2042 — in less than two generations — non-Latino, white Americans will no longer be a majority in the US. The process becomes irreversible long before that. It may already be irreversible.

This trend has far reaching political implications. The Democratic Party controlled by the New Left decided to take advantage of the situation. They formed an alliance with Latino activists to promote Hispanic immigration. Once Latinos joined the New Left coalition all other groups were required to accept them and their activists, no matter how extreme. This strategy was adopted all the way back during the Kennedy administration.

President Kennedy had an ambitious social agenda. Among other things he wanted to radically change American immigration policy. His assassination delayed this plan. His brother Senator Edward Kennedy introduced the legislation in 1965. Despite many promises to the contrary, the new law drastically changed the source countries where immigrants came from. European immigrants were largely replaced by Latin Americans and Asians. Later on Africans and Middle Easterners were added to the mix. As a result the ethnic make-up of the country significantly shifted in the following decades. Today, non-European immigrants represent an overwhelming majority of the foreign-born population.

Latinos are generally more diverse than African Americans. They originated from many different countries and settled in the US over a longer period. They came from much more disparate backgrounds, ranging from US citizens of Puerto Rico to refugees from communist Cuba. As a result, their political allegiances are also more varied. Even now, significant numbers of Hispanics vote Republican.

The issue of immigration, especially illegal immigration, changed the political equation. The right-wing got caught in a political trap. Accepting uncontrolled immigration will inevitably change the political equilibrium in favor of the Left. Newer and poorer immigrants will undoubtedly vote for politicians who offer them more government help, more welfare, more Socialism and more liberal immigration policies. Opposing illegal immigration, on the other hand, will alienate many Hispanics who otherwise might support the Republican Party.

Latinos have to choose between their ethnic kin and a prosperous America, between uncontrolled immigration and America as we know it. They seem to be choosing their ethnic kin in great numbers.

A careful examination of the history of the immigration conundrum clearly shows that this problem was not primarily caused by the Hispanic minority. It was carefully designed and deliberately constructed by the New Left.

It may still be possible to solve the immigration problem. It would require a convincing defeat of the New Left and a change of heart by a significant portion of the Latino community leadership.

7.8 — Radical Feminists

The entire known history of human kind is a sorry chronicle of oppression of women.

Ever since the first city states were established in ancient Mesopotamia women were mistreated. Not only were they denied equal rights with men, but they were often considered as property. Even today many different cultures approve of fathers selling their daughters for dowry, encourage female genital mutilation, force women to wear a *burqa*, forbid them to drive cars and so on.

Our own history is not much better. Not that long ago we burnt women as witches, we denied them the right to vote, the right to divorce, the right to an abortion and so on. Husbands were allowed to rape and beat their wives.

Not surprisingly, women fought against these injustices for centuries.

The feminist movement in Western Europe and North America started out in a sensible way. Women fought for equal rights, especially for voting rights. It is a sad commentary on men that it took more than five decades after the Civil War and the Emancipation Proclamation for women to gain the right to vote, and then only after a bitter fight.

The very nature of women's predicament determined their place in the political spectrum. Conservative society opposed their demands based on millennia of patriarchal tradition. Women had little choice: if they wanted to succeed they had to ally themselves with the left-wing. In early 20th Century America that meant the Progressive Movement.

Early Progressives fought against big business and monopolies, for social reform and more equality. They supported government regulation and public education. They encouraged the labor movement and enacted child labor laws. They promoted conservationism, an early version of environmentalism.

They sided with feminists in their fight for the right to vote and for prohibition of alcohol. These two goals were finally achieved by the enactment of the 18th and 19th Constitutional Amendments soon after the end of World War I.

Unfortunately, the support and fight for Prohibition backfired on women. Approximately one third of federal government revenues came from excise taxes on alcohol. The resulting loss of this revenue was replaced by the ever-increasing Federal Income Tax (instituted by the 16th Constitutional Amendment in 1909).

Prohibition proved to be very unpopular. Combined with the effects of the Great Depression and the Second World War this reversal in public opinion brought the feminist movement to a temporary halt.

With the rise of the New Left a second wave of feminism swept over America. This movement was far more liberating and far more radical than the first wave. It was also more sexual in nature, involving issues of birth control, sexual activity and abortion.

New Left feminism received significant boosts from Democratic Presidents. In 1961 President Kennedy's Executive Order 10980 established the Presidential Commission on the Status of Women. With his Executive Order 11246 President Johnson extended the benefits of Affirmative Action to women (and other minorities) in 1965.

This phase of the feminist movement was intimately connected with the New Left. The movement was accepted into the New Left coalition on the same conditions as all other groups. Feminists had to accept all other groups and their ideologies, no matter how extreme. As a result, feminism itself became more and more radical.

Paradoxically, improvement in the lives of women didn't help the feminist movement. Women, after all, are not really a minority in the same sense as African Americans or homosexuals are. In fact, there are more women than men in most countries (with the notable exception of China). Furthermore, women are not more inclined by nature to support the political Left, than men are. Economic dependence (raising children) and continued unfair disadvantages make them more supportive of social programs. None of this turns them into radicals in great numbers.

Nevertheless, the leadership of the feminist movement became more and more extreme. This was a direct result of the New Left's strategy and tactics. As the movement became increasingly radical, more and more women turned their backs on feminism. The movement was hollowed out and has shrunk to a relatively small group of radical activists. These activists still claim the right to represent all women on all issues. In reality, however, they are only agents of the extreme New Left.

Several New Left objectives are in direct contradiction with basic feminist values. As we have seen, when such conflicts arise the group involved is obliged to follow the 'greater good' and do whatever it can to hasten the destruction of capitalism and American imperialism. As a result, today we see the sorry spectacle of radical feminists completely abandoning crucial women's issues. Fundamentalist Islam is amongst the worst violators of women's rights. Yet, radical feminists are generally unwilling to denounce this most hideous oppressor of women. Radical feminists abandoned hundreds of millions of women in favor of 'class warfare'. They allied themselves with sworn enemies of America and betrayed their fellow women and their cause.

They reached the point where they actually ridicule the efforts of insufficiently radical feminists, mockingly calling them "*femmenists*". This is not the first time feminism became the victim of left-wing extremism. Orthodox Marxism, Stalinism, the Soviet Union and Antonio Gramsci all took advantage of legitimate demands of women.

7.9 — Gays - Homosexuals

Sexual morals and sexual morality were always contentious issues. Homosexuality more so. Only 20 pages into Genesis, the very first book of the Bible, God himself rained fire and brimstone on the city of Sodom on the account of widespread sodomy. He was particularly infuriated by local homosexuals who insisted on having sex with three of his Angels visiting Abraham on a divine mission. Both Judaism and Islam consider homosexuality a capital offense. Modern Catholicism, on the other hand, seems to support it, at least within its own ranks.

Any discussion of homosexuality is fraught with danger. Yet, it must be discussed as it plays a major role in today's political landscape. That is why AIDS is our Exhibit Number One.

The very definition of homosexuality is loaded with political and ideological significance. Depending on one's political convictions someone's sexual persuasion may look radically different.

From the Left, homosexuality is viewed as sexual *orientation*, a manifestation of one's *identity*. From the Right, it looks like abnormal sexual *behavior*, a deviancy in need of correction, a cure, and possibly punishment.

Gay people assert that homosexuality is not a choice but an essential and inborn part of their very nature, their very being. Social conservatives are convinced that homosexuality is just another aberration and gay people lie about it in order to cover up their sins.

So which one is it?

An impartial observer should consider both possibilities. Since neither can be ruled out categorically the subject should be thoroughly investigated. Carefully designed studies should be conducted; large amounts of data should be collected, verified and analyzed. Eventually, valid conclusions could be drawn. Alas, this seems to be impossible. Why?

Even without the benefit of such studies one could still formulate a hypothesis. It seems reasonable that both alternatives are entirely possible, indeed highly likely, very real. In the absence of absolute proof we have no choice but accept this hypothesis for now. If we don't, the entire issue will remain outside the reach of reason and left to be used as political football forever and ever.

Let us stipulate that some people are born gay. For whatever biological, genetic, hormonal or developmental reason(s), they are, by their very nature, sexually and emotionally attracted to people of the same sex. At the present level of scientific development there is nothing anyone can do to change this fact. (Whether anyone should even try is another difficult question. For now, we will go with the assumption that no one should try to change any such inborn preference.)

Let us also stipulate that some people who were not born gay may develop homosexual behavior later on. This may happen due to their circumstances, such as long periods of isolation from members of the other sex. This is still a fairly common experience for many people, in boarding schools, in the military, in prisons, nunneries, madrassas, etc. Economic obstacles of acquiring a mate are also widespread in the Third World. It may also happen due to chance sexual encounters with gay people. Sexual pleasure is a strong motivator regardless of its source.

We have no way of knowing what percentage of gay people were born that way. Further clouding the issue is the tendency of people to rationalize their actions. Looking back, a chance homosexual encounter may seem like destiny, an essential part of one's self. This is especially so when a strong social reinforcement mechanism is at work. And there is. We regularly witness the joyful celebration of someone "coming out" as gay. The implication, of course, is that he/she was always gay, just chose to conceal this fact, probably for fear of discrimination. We never hear of anyone who became gay. We never hear of anyone going into the closet. We never hear of anyone who became addicted to homosexual behavior.

Why is this important?

There is strength in numbers and the gay community needs strength. Some minorities are given. You are either black or you are not. You cannot really become black, although you can fake it. Other minorities are more elastic. Some religions are like that. You can readily convert to Christianity or Islam, and with some difficulty to Judaism. Homosexuality is somewhere in between. One can easily become gay simply by practicing homosexuality. For the gay community and especially for gay activists every homosexual person is an asset. The more openly so, the higher the value.

Homosexuals were prosecuted through much of history. Some societies were more tolerant than others, but being homosexual was almost always detrimental. Understandably, gay people (regardless of their origins) went to great lengths to hide their sexual preference. Becoming homosexual was never advantageous until very recently.

Puritanical traditions made the lives of American gays hell. They were despised, prosecuted and harassed through much of our history. Being identified as homosexual usually ended one's career. Fathers routinely disowned their gay sons. Wives divorced their gay husbands. Families ostracized their gay members. Shame, rejection, humiliation, violence, blackmail was common against gay people, especially gay men.

Following Antonio Gramsci's suggestion the New Left offered an alliance to homosexuals. At the beginning progress was slow. They had to fight deep-seated prejudices in an overwhelmingly hostile social environment. Homosexuality was considered a crime in many parts of the country and the world.

The sexual revolution brought significant improvements. Society, especially young people, became much more tolerant. The gay liberation movement quickly gathered steam. Conservative social forces reacted by increasing the pressure. Police regularly raided gay bars. Meanwhile, American society experienced a series of major upheavals. During the 1960-s the US was engulfed by anti-war demonstrations, campus violence and race riots. Finally, on June 28, 1969 homosexuals had their very own riot. For the first time ever in America gay people fought back against oppression. A police raid on a New York City gay bar named Stonewall Inn led to a violent reaction.

With some help from other leftist groups the gay liberation movement finally prevailed. The police backed off. The Stonewall Riots were a decisive turning point in the gay rights movement. The next decade was the golden age of gay sexuality in America. Gay people seemed to be everywhere, especially in big cities, having sex wherever and whenever they felt like it. Life was full of pleasure and the future seemed exceedingly bright.

All that abruptly ended with the appearance of AIDS. The sexual revolution was suddenly over. (See Exhibit One.)

AIDS very nearly destroyed the gay community of the United States. The mortality rates were shockingly high. There was no cure. No one even knew what caused the disease. No reliable test was available; there was no way to know if one was infected. It was entirely possible that everyone was already infected and would soon die a terrible death. Homosexuals once again became outcasts.

The gay community needed help. Miraculously, help materialized. The New Left political machine geared up and responded magnificently. Activists of all stripes volunteered to help. It was social activism at its most efficient. The leaders took a huge risk but at the end their efforts paid off big.

A united New Left mounted one of the most effective propaganda efforts ever seen. It was masterfully crafted, efficiently delivered and overwhelming. For homosexuals AIDS activism was literally a matter of life and death. So they gave everything they've got to the effort. By the time they were done every single belief regarding AIDS was overturned. AIDS was no longer a gay disease. AIDS was a viral infection not an STD (Sexually Transmitted Disease). Its name was changed from GRID to AIDS to HIV-AIDS, emphasizing the virus. Homosexuals were victims of the disease, and victims only, not agents of it. Billions of dollars were poured into research to develop tests, cures and vaccines. Discriminating against AIDS sufferers became illegal. Immigration restrictions against AIDS infected people were rescinded. Celebrities rallied around the cause. AIDS walks and AIDS support marches became regular charity events. In 1990 Congress passed the Ryan White CARE Act, named after a young boy who contracted AIDS through blood transfusion (a rare occurrence). The new law provided for federally funded health care for people with AIDS. People who developed cancer as a complication of AIDS, which they acquired through anal sex, received preferential treatment over people who developed cancer the conventional way.

Slowly the medical situation also improved. Tests were formulated. The HIV virus was isolated. Effective treatments were developed. AIDS in America and in other industrialized countries was no longer an immediate death sentence.

The gay community recovered. At first the revival was slow and uncertain but once the mortal danger passed it became very powerful. All the energy invested in the movement paid off. The survivors harvested extraordinarily rich benefits. The entire social structure seems to have changed. The activists turned all their energy against the remains of discrimination. They demanded full acceptance and an honorable place in society.

It was a relentless drive. Newly enacted laws prohibited any and all discrimination. Speaking out against gays or homosexuality became risky. Retribution was quick and often devastating. Bastions of old social traditions were attacked and destroyed one by one. Hollywood was the first to fall. Today gay characters proliferate in movies, TV shows and theatre. They are invariably cast in favorable light, unlike business leaders, corporations or the military. Gays secured the right to teach in schools and to adopt children. They are rapidly advancing in many other sectors of society, in business, in religion and in government. The expression "...the first openly gay..." became both a rallying cry and a declaration of victory.

The movement was no longer fighting against oppression or even discrimination. The full acceptance and normalization of gay lifestyle became the new objective. Mainstreaming homosexuality is within reach.

Even after all the successes gay activists still have a full agenda. They want gay marriage to become a full reality, equal in all respects to heterosexual marriage. They want full acceptance of gay identity and gay behavior by the US military. They want schools to portray homosexuality every bit as normal as heterosexuality. There is still a lot of resistance out there from ordinary people. But victory seems inevitable, only a few Supreme Court decisions away.

The New Left had won another tremendous victory. The vision Antonio Gramsci saw in his prison seems to be vindicated. The two decades long offensive forged an unbreakable alliance between the New Left and the homosexual community. Their leaderships are fused together. Gay liberation is one of the most successful movements the Left has ever embarked upon.

Is there anything wrong with this? Just ask the other side.

It is highly questionable that promoting homosexuality is a positive or even healthy development. The entire idea rests upon unproven assumptions. We have no way of knowing how natural, how normal, how healthy homosexual behavior really is, especially in the long run. No society has ever developed along the lines proposed by gay activists. AIDS is still primarily transmitted by male homosexual intercourse. The disease is not under control by any measure and the virus can mutate into a much more lethal pathogen at any time. AIDS is still very much an epidemic in much of the Third World. Many millions are infected and die a terrible death.

Society has been forced to tolerate many of these changes. Reluctant submission, however, is not the same as voluntary acceptance. Much of society is fed up with changes imposed on it by left-wing activists, legislators, government agencies and judges. A major backlash is entirely possible and even likely.

All constituent forces of the New Left are led and controlled by the most extreme elements of the movement. This is true for the gay community as well. Left to their own devices most gay people would settle down to live ordinary lives. They should be allowed to live as they want as long as they don't harm anyone. Sex should be a private matter between consenting adults, nothing more and nothing less.

To understand the dangers of mixing sex and power, homosexuality with ideology, we only need to look at the pedophile priests of the Catholic Church. Most of them are homosexuals who used their power over little boys to satisfy their carnal desires. They are protected by an organization mainly concerned with its own power and privileges.

Militant homosexuality is fraught with extreme danger. Sodomy in the privacy of one's bedroom is one thing, practicing sodomy as a political act in public is quite another. Politically sodomizing an unwilling public is unwise in the extreme.

7.10 — Environmentalists

Everybody loves the environment. Environmentalists believe otherwise. They are convinced that sinister forces, especially business people, are hell bent on destroying the planet. Some environmentalists believe that business people do this simply because they are greedy, while others consider capitalism an evil system and capitalists as agents of willful destruction.

Ordinary people enjoy the goods produced by agriculture and industry. They also like clean air and water, wild animals and national parks, sandy beaches, beautiful flowers, waterfalls and forests. They understand that there is a tradeoff between these values, and competing interests must be balanced if humanity is to survive and thrive.

To be sure, we must be vigilant protecting nature. It is all too easy to ignore the environmental damage we cause as we are trying to grow more food and manufacture more products. Throughout history we cut down forests for firewood and timber, we cleared jungles for agriculture, we polluted lakes and rivers with human, animal and industrial waste, we choked our cities and villages with air pollution and we devastated other species of animals. In fact, we killed off the mammoth and other mega fauna as soon as we figured out how. Native Americans hunted the horse to extinction in North America.

On the other hand, America has more forests now than back in the 17th Century, our air and our water is cleaner than it has ever been since the Industrial Revolution began.

Caring for the environment is a noble goal. Nature conservation, protecting endangered species, keeping our waters and air clean are worthwhile goals. Most people realize that achieving these objectives is a hard task and an expensive undertaking. We are willing to pay the costs. We build water treatment plants, we install catalytic converters in our cars, we recycle our waste, we donate money to save the whales, we appreciate our park rangers and we feed the birds, the squirrels and deer.

For most of the last two centuries nature conservation was uncontroversial. We were far from perfect, our actions were often questionable and contradictory, but we tried hard and we made good, constant progress. Both political parties agreed to the basic principles.

Things started to change in the 1960-s. At the beginning it was almost imperceptible. It started with books. The very first one was *Silent Spring* written by Rachel Carson. Originally, it was serialized in *The New Yorker* magazine in 1962. A few months later it was published in book form with an unusual endorsement by William O. Douglas, a leftist US Supreme Court Justice appointed by FDR.

Silent Spring was a blanket indictment of pesticides. President Kennedy used the book as an excuse to order an investigation of the chemical industry. The newly formed Environmental Defense Fund filed a lawsuit to ban DDT. Eventually, the courts forced the federal government (EPA) to ban the pesticide. Soon many other countries followed suit.

Other books followed. Some were concerned with population growth, others with economic growth. The movement quickly branched out to encompass all fashionable ideologies. The New Left was involved from the very beginning. Environmentalism became a political movement, a militant anti-growth and anti-capitalism dogma.

In 1979 the Three Mile Island nuclear power plant in Pennsylvania suffered a partial meltdown. It was a serious accident but not a catastrophe. Some radioactive gases were released into the atmosphere but there were no casualties and only minimal health effects. By chance, just a couple of weeks before the accident the motion picture *The China Syndrome* was released, starring Jane Fonda. The movie was about a nuclear power plant accident.

Environmental activists and the media had a field day. Countless anti-nuclear demonstrations were held all over America. Soon the United States stopped building nuclear power plants. Numerous reactors were shut down and many previously ordered plants were cancelled. Billions of dollars were wasted. The activists smelled blood. The New Left had another battle cry: "No Nukes!" And there were no nukes.

Many new environmental laws were enacted. Government agencies were created to regulate everything remotely connected with the environment. Activist organizations proliferated. The United Nations got involved. Conferences were held. Earth Day was celebrated. Greenpeace was organized. Congress mandated the promotion of environmental education. Much of the New Left's environmental agenda effortlessly mutated into taxpayer funded government programs.

There was a sense of accomplishment in the air. Environmentalism triumphed.

This was bad news for the New Left. They didn't mind the victory but they wanted a continuous fight, a *permanent revolution*. They needed a constantly growing and active movement against capitalism. To keep the environmental crusade going required a new villain, a new threat, a dangerous enemy.

Global Warming was born in 1988. The father of the newborn was a NASA scientist named James E. Hansen. Up until then the concept was almost completely unknown except for a 'prophecy' uttered in the 1973 science fiction movie *Soylent Green*. Interestingly, the film bears a striking resemblance to the hellish vision of today's environmentalist propaganda. We can probably thank Frank R. Bowerman for this vision. As a technical advisor on the movie he was responsible for making predictions of what New York City would be like in the year 2022. Surprisingly, he doesn't even have a Wikipedia page.

Others were tinkering with the concept of "greenhouse effect" as far back as 1979.

Global Warming serves the same ideological purpose as the biblical Apocalypse and Judgment Day. It predicts the end of the world. It describes Mother Earth dying a slow and painful death because of the sins of humans. Overpopulation, economic growth, industry and civilization are blamed for this terrible catastrophe. Humans are urged to mend their ways before it's too late.

This time, however, Armageddon is not a divine prophecy; it is 'scientific certainty' (much like Karl Marx's theory of social progress and class warfare). Nevertheless, it has all the necessary ingredients any high priest could hope for in a well-crafted religion. It provides only one way to escape certain annihilation: the immediate and complete destruction of capitalism. Like all religions, it is preached ferociously and constantly. It is a proselytizing creed.

Global Warming is a perfect bogeyman. It neatly ties agriculture, industrial production and energy usage to greenhouse gases, which in turn destroy the planet. Just before the Global Warming scare there was the new ice-age hysteria. Nuclear war was destined to cause nuclear winter. Earth was certain to freeze. This idea was soon discarded, however. Freezing temperatures called for heating, for more energy, for production and all of these were beneficial to capitalism. The new ice-age monster was counterproductive. Soon it was replaced by a much more anti-capitalist Global Warming monster.

Within two decades from its humble beginnings Global Warming grew into a multinational powerhouse, a media empire, a money machine and a political juggernaut. Billions of dollars were spent by governments and industry on greenhouse gas research. Nobel Prizes and Oscars have been awarded to its high priests. But the essence of it still remains a dogmatic ideology with a well-defined political objective.

Amongst all the ideologically motivated groups within the New Left alliance environmentalists are the most pure. The activists have no ulterior motives. They serve no self-interests. They know not what they are doing and why.

Their leaders, of course, know exactly what they are doing. They are wielding one of the deadliest weapons known to mankind, the weapon of zealotry. The only other comparable ideology in existence today is global Jihad waged by fundamentalist Islam.

Scientific zealotry is an oxymoron. The science of Global Warming is highly questionable. Recent revelations prove that the methods, the motivations and the actions of so-called climate scientists are all very much suspect. Climate science is the twin brother of scientific materialism and scientific socialism. It is political ideology masquerading as science.

7.11 — Journalists — Media

Journalists occupy a special position in society. They are professionals who operate the mass media, the industry that controls the distribution of news and other information. They are at the center of power — where politics, entertainment, news, information, ideology and public opinion intersect. As professionals, they have their own distinct self-interests (see later). As activists they serve political purposes.

The profession of journalism attracts people with a certain temperament. Journalists tend to be sensitive to suffering and injustice; they value egalitarian ideas and 'social progress'.

Various political groups always tried to control or at least influence 'the press', or the media as it is now known. As a result, disinterested objective journalism was always very precious and it rarely survived for long. Despite the natural inclinations of journalists, stable or oppressive political systems generally managed to develop a compliant press.

Only free and democratic societies can have a free press. Indeed, such societies **must** have a free press if they wish to remain free. Oppressing people always entails controlling the media. Getting the upper hand in a power struggle often involves taking control of the press, or at least suppressing it. Revolutionary movements always try to influence, manipulate or even dominate the press.

Ideologically based powers need to control information as much as possible. In such situations propaganda and information become indistinguishable. Ideological powers have a tendency to become totalitarian, as do military powers. Catholicism (inquisition), Bolshevism, Nazism, Stalinism and Maoism are examples of such tendencies. Often the first sign of trouble for such powers is their loss of information monopoly.

Marxism, as an ideologically driven revolutionary movement, recognized the importance of journalists and the press. Many early Marxists were journalists or became journalists as part of their activism. Marxist parties always had an Agitation and Propaganda Department, known as *AgitProp,* even at the cell level, at the very bottom of the party hierarchy. Disseminating true and accurate information was never their goal.

Antonio Gramsci also recognized the importance of the press. Journalists were assigned a special role in his scheme to achieve *cultural hegemony*. He also recognized the usefulness of other 'media professionals', although much of these media and the term itself have not yet been invented. Nevertheless, he understood the importance that culture and the arts played in society and social conflict.

The New Left learnt how to manipulate information from past masters. They studied Marx and Engels, Lenin and Stalin, Hitler and Goebbels, Mao Zedong and Fidel Castro, William Randolph Hearst and Joseph Pulitzer. They analyzed the English Civil War and the American and French Revolutions. They also understood the value of subtle propaganda disguised as art.

Journalism and publishing are traditionally capital intensive industries. To establish and run a newspaper, to publish and distribute books in a meaningful and relevant way always required a lot of money. Amongst the 'aristocracy' of American cities we invariably find the families who established the first newspapers in their communities. The need for capital is one of the main reasons why *freedom of the press* is distinct from *freedom of speech;* why it is a specifically enumerated right in the First Amendment of the US Constitution.

This need for capital also ensured that by and large the press was always part of the establishment. *Freedom of the press* enabled American Marxists to publish the *Daily Worker,* but the huge overhead costs ensured that most newspapers were distributed by mainstream publishers and were read by ordinary citizens. As American capitalism thrived newspaper publishing became big business. 'Publishing empires' were born concentrating control over many newspapers and book publishing companies in a few hands. Accordingly, most publications were conservative.

Eventually, most publishing companies sold stock to the public and thus became publicly held corporations (see chapter 4.6 above). Even then, most original owners or their families effectively retained control over these enterprises. As generations passed their control gradually loosened up. At the same time the descendants of the founding publishers moved to the Left politically. This is a common phenomenon amongst heirs of great fortunes. These processes accelerated under the organized onslaught of the New Left.

New Left theorists designated *the press* and education as their primary takeover targets. Seizing control over journalism schools were like hitting two birds with one stone. Newly minted, overwhelmingly left-wing journalism graduates flooded the newspaper industry. For a while they had to work for conservative editors and publishers, but they rose up through the ranks very quickly. Within a decade most of the American press became decidedly left-wing oriented.

Other forms of media were even more vulnerable. Radio and television were much better suited for political manipulation than ordinary newspapers. It was much easier to implant a political message into stories presented in images and sounds. Television became a major mouthpiece of New Left propaganda. Interestingly, radio turned out differently. To this day talk-radio is a major headache for the Left.

Eventually, the New Left managed to take control of several media companies. Today New Left activists actually run some these corporations, they sit on their boards of directors, they are CEO-s and division heads. Huge media conglomerates usually own newspapers, magazines, movie studios, book and music publishers and TV channels. Capable executives of these corporations have total control over the *message* conveyed by the various types of media produced by company divisions. Not surprisingly, most media producing enterprises serve a decidedly left-wing agenda.

The rise of the Internet shook up the media business. Capital intensiveness that concentrated control in a few hands significantly diminished. Very large media empires lost their footing under pressure from the new competition. They suddenly lost the ability to make a profit by gathering and distributing information. When unlimited quantities of propaganda is given away for free, fewer and fewer people are willing to pay for it. The serious decline of profitability significantly damaged the infrastructure. Paid reporters became an expensive luxury few companies could afford.

Centralized control of the Media disappeared. The Main Stream Media (MSM) is still tightly controlled but its share of information distribution is steadily shrinking. Journalists and other Media professionals are still overwhelmingly left-wing but their control is fading. The entire field is in a constant flux. The jury is still out on the final outcome of this power struggle.

We can make one important and interesting observation: the democratization and liberalization of the Media did not favor liberals and left-wing activists. This indicates an imbalance between the supply and demand for left-wing propaganda. People are not buying what the New Left is selling, certainly not in the quantities produced and offered. Absent a distribution monopoly propaganda is a much harder sell.

The effects of breaking up the Media monopoly are instructive for other professional monopolies. (See the chapters on the various professional classes.)

7.12 — Demagoguery

Demagoguery is as old as democracy itself.

It is a tactic employed by politicians and others to generate support for various causes by appealing to the emotions of the public. Originally, the word meant a leader of the 'common people' who are easily swayed by lies, half-truths and emotional appeals for (often violent) action. Demagoguery is a form of propaganda which often utilizes real or imagined insults and abuses that a particular group finds offensive.

Demagoguery — as all propaganda — is used in all societies, regardless of what form of government they have. Democracies, however, are more vulnerable to demagogues than societies with any other type of government. This is because in a democracy politicians need the support and the votes of the people to stay in office. In most other societies passive acceptance (not rioting) is sufficient to keep the rulers in power. Therefore, demagoguery is far more sophisticated in democratic societies than anywhere else. This is especially so in countries with long democratic traditions, such as the USA.

All sides of the political continuum use demagoguery to some extent. Movements based on ideology use it more than others, simply because they trade in abstractions and ideas rather than observable facts or raw power.

The New Left is a masterful practitioner of demagoguery. They have to be as their entire agenda is based on deception, including their goals, their methods, their motivations, everything.

The New Left developed custom-made propaganda for each group it targets. New Left theorists have created a ready-made arsenal of vocabulary, slogans, stories, arguments, etc. for each minority targeted for recruitment into *Minority Bolshevism*. Political correctness and multiculturalism are also part of this weaponry. Radical activists of each minority — the community organizers — use these weapons with ease, gracefully and convincingly misleading their 'brothers and sisters'.

Thus, we have racial demagoguery, feminist demagoguery, 'pro-choice' demagoguery, class warfare demagoguery, union demagoguery, gay demagoguery, welfare demagoguery, environmental demagoguery, Islamic demagoguery, anti-American demagoguery, anti-Zionist demagoguery, and so on.

Demagoguery is a very effective weapon used by political power against economic power. Notice how the front lines are defined: capitalists are invariably described as greedy bankers and heartless CEO-s outsourcing jobs to China and India. They are never acknowledged as creators of wealth and providers of jobs.

The cutting edge of the New Left's demagoguery project is practiced under laboratory conditions constantly measuring the feedback received both from the already faithful and from potential converts. Let us briefly examine some of these demagoguery laboratories.

7.13 — Humogoguery

This newly coined word refers to various comedy shows regularly shown on television. Over time these shows evolved into highly effective New Left propaganda machines. They mix actual comedy (often, but not always, very funny, high quality comedy) with thinly disguised propaganda presented in a supposedly funny, humorous way. These propaganda pieces are well-designed mass-produced skits. They use ridicule (often blatantly unfairly) instead of real humor on their subject matters and on targeted individuals. There are observable humogoguery 'algorithms'.

Sometimes these *comedia*ns target democratic politicians. This enables them to claim that they are not partisan, but rather equal opportunity offenders. They forget to mention that they always criticize all their targets from a radical far-left point of view. Ideologically, they are very biased, indeed. They just hide their *humogoguery* behind more demagoguery.

Several of these 'comedy shows' became very effective tools in converting clueless and impressionable youths who have been well prepared for this role by another New Left group: the education professionals.

Some of these comedians are very talented. They are clearly qualified to be members of the very prestigious group of master propagandists of nascent totalitarian powers. They are regularly awarded various entertainment awards for their efforts.

7.14 — Scientogoguery

As we have seen, Marxism always strived to be recognized as a science. Both Soviet Bolshevism and the New Left kept up this tradition. All self-respecting Marxist leaders wanted to prove their mastery of "scientific socialism" by contributing to the theory. Even Stalin felt the need to publish 'theoretical' books.

This scientism fetish was put to further use in certain New Left projects. Claims of 'scientific proof' of New Left positions proved very effective and persuasive in particular projects and to particular targeted minorities.

To various extent this *scientism* shows up in many different fields. Most of these efforts were made in social and political sciences and economics.

Scientific claims of the Left (both old and new) eventually invaded even real natural sciences. Scientific battles were fought over the existence and measurement of intelligence (IQ) as part of the effort to scientifically prove racial and gender equality. Battles were fought in biology and genetics to prove that homosexuality was not a choice. Vicious scientific wars were fought over the nature of AIDS and HIV. Scientific crusades were waged against the tobacco industry and against selected other businesses and companies, such as pharmaceuticals, various foods and food additives, asbestos, etc.

Of course, ideologically based attacks on science are nothing new. What is new, however, is the ideological infiltration of science, the corruption of science and scientists from the inside for ideological reasons, the misuse of science for political gain.

In the past we witnessed the Catholic Church making a frontal attack on Galileo and his scientific discoveries only to lose this fight in the long run (highly embarrassing). In the present we are witnessing the New Left attacking economic power with ideologically based arguments disguised as science.

Nowhere is this *scientogoguery* (another newly coined word) more evident than in radical environmentalism, especially in the study of Global Warming.

7.15 — Ecogoguery

In fact, 'global warming science' deserves its very own word: *ecogoguery*. In the same vein, homosexual demagoguery could be called *homogoguery* (this word has been used previously by others).

The study of complex phenomena — especially social phenomena — is not science. One can study history, the weather, earthquakes, the stock market, horse racing, art or popular culture but such studies are not science. Some of these studies may contain scientific elements, such as archeology, thermodynamics, geology, horse biology, or the physics of sound or color, but there is no history science, weather science, earthquake science, stock market science, horse racing science, art science or culture science.

Man-made Global Warming is not a scientific hypothesis. It is an ideological, political agenda dressed up in pseudo-scientific drag paddled by New Left agitators masquerading as scientists or by actual scientists who are betrayers of true science.

Man-made Global Warming cannot be verified and it cannot be falsified.

Numerous fraudulent practices were discovered and proven beyond any reasonable doubt in the Global Warming project. Data was altered, objections were silenced, dissenters were penalized, critics were demonized, publications were censored, and careers were ruined by agents of the New Left. The Catholic Church's attack on Galileo was just as misguided but it was far more honest on a much smaller scale.

When the truth finally came out the entire New Left movement, all of Minority Bolshevism came to the rescue. The most vocal defenders of *ecogoguery* were the celebrity hit men, the practitioners of *humogoguery,* ridiculing every concern, every objection and every dissenter.

7.16 — Anti-Americanism

The history of Communism is intimately linked with empires. Its chief theorists Karl Marx and Friedrich Engels (bona-fide dead white males) lived in England and wrote their most important works in the British Empire. The *Communist Manifesto* was first published in London. Prussian Emperor Kaiser Wilhelm II dispatched Lenin and his Bolshevik allies (all dead white males) to make revolution against his enemy, the Czar of Russia, who was his cousin. Communism finally triumphed on the ruins of the Russian Empire. Eventually, the Soviet Union itself became a very powerful empire. Mao Zedong fought against the Chinese Empire as a young man.

Thus, it is not surprising that the communist movement was always preoccupied by imperialism. Lenin himself declared *Imperialism, the Highest Stage of Capitalism* in 1916, as World War I was raging. He did not invent the idea, however. Both concepts of imperialism and anti-imperialism already existed back in the 19th Century. The current concepts of imperialism and anti-imperialism, however, did originate with Lenin and the Bolshevik Revolution.

After World War II Stalin (another dead white male) quickly built up the Soviet Empire. At the same time he declared the United States, the 'American Empire' the number one enemy of the working classes of the entire world. His successors followed his lead and adopted anti-imperialism as one of the cornerstones of their ideology.

Imperialism quickly became synonymous with American Imperialism. Accordingly, anti-imperialism became synonymous with anti-Americanism. Expansionist Soviet policies attempted to turn all newly independent Third World countries against America. They were largely successful. Communism was on the march everywhere, in Africa, South East Asia, China, Latin America and Eastern Europe.

Anti-Americanism became one of the central tenets of Soviet ideology and Third World Marxism. Every two-bit dictator on Soviet payroll was a proud anti-American hero. Fidel Castro was worshipped by both the international and the American left. Che Guevara was deified. Bona-fide intellectuals were expected to be anti-Americans, everywhere, even in America. *Useful idiots* eagerly complied. No demonstration was considered complete without burning American flags. The Weather Underground declared war on America.

After the collapse of Communism the Soviet Empire was no more. Yet, despite America's victory, anti-Americanism survived and strived. The ghost of Marxist ideology, the "spectre of Communism" was still "haunting Europe" and the rest of the world. Nobody seemed to be able "to exorcise this spectre". Not everybody wanted to.

The United States of America is the biggest enemy of the Left (both old and new). The US is not only the biggest power, the only remaining superpower, but it is also a personification of capitalism. Its very power, its wealth is a refutation of Marxist ideology. The New Left can only be victorious over the dead body of America. No US, no capitalism.

Thus, the deep seated hatred for America is a cornerstone of New Left ideology. The USA must be constantly criticized, vilified, damned, and ultimately it must be defeated and destroyed. America serves the same purpose for the New Left as the devil does for the Church.

Anti-Americanism has another, practical use. It provides a convenient common ground with enemies of all stripes of the United States. Anti-Americanism (together with anti-Zionism) enables the New Left to establish a common cause with forces it has nothing in common with. Anti-Americanism makes it possible for the New Left to form alliances with countries and political forces that are ideologically incompatible with core components of Minority Bolshevism.

Women are oppressed by Islam. Homosexuals are executed and jailed in Muslim countries. Abortion is forbidden by the Catholic Church. Janjaweed militias are massacring Sudanese blacks. China produces more greenhouse gases than any other country. Yet, they all have one thing in common: the hatred of America. They all vote together in the United Nations to denounce the US. The New

Left cheers them on. Countless newspaper articles, hundreds of books and dozens of movies condemn America, year after year, decade after decade.

American (and foreign) moviegoers are no longer surprised to see our enemies depicted as heroic victims who fight US forces, the CIA, greedy capitalists, evil corporations, ruthless businessmen, and so on.

Leftist media go out of their way to portray minorities, illegal aliens, criminals, anti-American activists and even self-confessed terrorists with compassion, in a positive light. The rest of us deserve no empathy and can expect no mercy.

7.17 — Common Patterns

A common thread is clearly visible in the history of relationships between minorities and the Left (both old and new).

All minorities had legitimate complaints against society, against the majority. They were oppressed, taken advantage of, treated unfairly and exploited. They were ignored and marginalized.

This abuse continued for centuries, generation after generation. Sometimes the victims fought back, mostly to be defeated. Any progress was slow and painful.

Throughout history various forces hostile to the majority in power took advantage of this simmering resentment and hostility. Outside powers often used the grievances of subjugated or enslaved populations for their own purposes. This strategy frequently worked. People who "have nothing to lose but their chains" can be very hazardous to their rulers. Of course, these confrontations rarely resulted in the liberation of the oppressed. Usually, the oppressed ended up serving a new master, who might or might not have proved to be better than the old one.

Occasionally, genuine revolutionary movements developed. Indigenous activists organized their downtrodden compatriots against their tormentors. Spartacus led a slave rebellion; the Jews revolted against Rome; the peasants waged war against the Holy Roman Empire. The American Revolution triumphed against the British Empire. The French Revolution succeeded for a time.

Rarely, ideologically motivated movements evolved. Some of them were victorious. They should be studied thoroughly, especially now, as we seem to be in the middle of just such a development. The most relevant examples were the rise and spread of Christianity, Islam, Buddhism, the Protestant Reformation, Nazism and the Bolshevik Revolutions in Russia and China.

We can observe similar patterns in our own history. We have oppressed and persecuted our racial minorities, women and homosexuals for centuries. We have exploited various worker groups to our advantage. There is no going around these facts.

So far, we have been lucky that no outside force has been able to take full advantage of these situations up till now. We have also been lucky that slavery was not a nationwide institution. Even the territorially limited version cost us dearly. The Civil War, reconstruction and perpetual racial unrest were all direct consequences of acts of historical wrongs, evil deeds, stupid mistakes and shortsighted policies.

Marxism has tried to take advantage of our mistakes and misdeeds. Again, we were lucky, mainly because Marxism was too rigid and too ignorant to see its way to victory. But our enemies are learning. Every injury we inflicted, every injustice we administered, every sin we committed and every insult we dealt will be used against us.

These injuries, injustices, sins and insults enabled our enemies to establish a foothold deep inside our society.

They agitate against us relentlessly. Every mistake we make helps them push further into our domain.

An important question must be answered. If we have really committed all these sinful acts how dare we call New Left ideology the enemy of the American people? If we were wrong aren't they right? If we were bad aren't they good? If we hurt people won't they help them?

No, no, no and no. Why not?

Just look at the common patterns hidden behind the policies of the New Left. Just look at history.

They find a disgruntled minority. They carefully analyze the grievances suffered by that minority. They express their outrage at the injustices, they convey their sense of sorrow and they promise reparations for the injuries and retributions against the perpetrators. They point to capitalism as the root cause of their suffering. They explain that all suffering is caused by capitalism and by the United States of America.

They personalize their diagnoses for the tastes of the targeted minority. They always assign guilt to the same group, but they put the emphasis on different attributes that resonate with each victim.

For African Americans the villain is the white man. For Latinos it's the Anglos. For women it's the patriarchal white male society. For gays it's straight whites. For the environmentalists it's capitalism and industry. For sensitive intellectual types it's the culture of "dead white males" (excluding all Marxists and Leftists). And so on.

Next, they offer a solution to remedy the situation. First the minority must be organized. New Left activists formulate an action plan, select the leaders, write a platform, issue press releases, hold meetings, demand action, write letters to Congress, etc.

Before long a new and radical leadership takes control of the minority movement. They prioritize the goals which gradually become more and more extreme.

Invariably, the newly ordained leaders declare war on their number one enemy, capitalism and its principal representative America. They are no different from any other group that took advantage of disgruntled minorities for their own benefit. For proof just look at history.

In Africa virtually all sub-Saharan countries became independent shortly after World War Two. Leftist regimes supported by the Soviet Union took control of the continent. Two generations later all of these countries are economic basket cases. Civil wars, famine, genocide, poverty, environmental catastrophes and disease are endemic. Naturally, the Left blames colonialism and capitalism for all of Africa's problems. But capitalist countries poured billions of dollars of aid into these countries. Leftist governments wasted almost all the money and stole the rest.

Fidel Castro's socialist revolution devastated Cuba. Soviet and Chinese Communism helped North Korea to establish a 'people's paradise'. East Germany's development was stunted by Communism. In two generations they managed to get three generations behind West Germany. They had to convert the country into a prison to keep their own people from escaping from their socialist utopia.

7.18 — Economically Motivated Groups

The New Left managed to assemble all ideologically motivated groups sympathetic to leftist causes into a single camp. It was an impressive feat. Armies of angry young people certain in their beliefs, convinced of the rightness of their causes were willing to fight. Still, it was not enough. Ideologically motivated groups only represented a minority of voters. All disgruntled minorities put together were still only a minority. A large minority, but still only a minority. It was painfully clear that the New Left would never be able to gather enough votes to win elections without mustering much more public support.

Sure, they could go on agitating, trying to convince more and more people to vote for them. But they knew that most people were not politically motivated. Most people just wanted a good life, security and prosperity. They also liked their freedom, and preferred to be left alone. Furthermore, prosperity was the result of economic activity and that was the domain of their number one enemy: economic power. Most people instinctively knew that prosperity was a product of capitalism. Most people liked prosperity.

What to do?

For a while they experimented with old methods. They tried to revive working class solidarity of the New Deal by courting blue collar unions. But both the economy and society had changed. The working class of the assembly line was shrinking and aging. Furthermore, many unionized workers didn't much care for activists and intellectuals, not to mention hippies, homosexuals and troublemakers. They mostly cared about their paychecks, their working conditions, their vacations and their pensions. A dependable majority of the shrinking blue-collar working class always voted for the Left. Even with their support the numbers were nowhere near enough.

The New Left had to look elsewhere for coalition partners. They had to look outside their traditional power base. A democratic, prosperous America was not easy to conquer from the Left. So they searched, plotted and strategized until they finally found what they were looking for at the most unlikely of places.

This momentous discovery changed everything.

7.19 — The Rise of New Labor

As we have seen above *labor unions* originally were based on economic power. Their most effective weapon was the strike, the ability to disrupt industrial production. In the beginning all they had was this economic power, as the political power (the government) usually sided with the employers, the capitalists who controlled the economy. This was always very obvious; as soon the strikers violated the owners' property rights with tactics such as sit-down strikes, occupying factories or blockading entrances the government intervened on behalf of the owners. Sometimes the police actually shot and killed the strikers.

Labor was always at a disadvantage in these fights as they were up against combined economic and political powers. Understandably, labor unions sought political allies from the very beginning of this conflict. Sometimes these efforts paid off, mostly in local contexts.

FDR's New Deal forever changed the relationship between industrial labor and capital. At the time this relationship was in an upheaval all over the world. This was partly due to the effects of the Great Depression, but also due to widespread social changes brought about by the collapse of empires in the wake of World War One. Both fascism and Soviet Bolshevism tried to use the labor unions for their own political ends with some success.

American labor unions eagerly grasped the political power offered them by FDR. This was not surprising if we consider that the Great Depression essentially eliminated all their economic power. There were millions of unemployed willing to work for less.

Twenty years of New Deal Socialism firmly embedded the labor unions in the political power structure. They became reliable allies of the Democratic Party. They mostly used their newfound political power to extract economic advantages for their members. They were so successful in these efforts that eventually they priced themselves out of competition. Global competition and cheap foreign labor wreaked havoc in traditional American industry which was forced to outsource much of its production to overseas. This immense economic dislocation ushered in the long decline of traditional American labor unions along with the decline of traditional American industries.

At the same time the New Left gradually took control of the Democratic Party. As part of their "long march through the institutions" they also took control of the labor unions. These hollowed-out unions became more and more radical and political. At the same time they all but lost their economic power. After more than a decade of contentious labor relations and constant strikes this loss of economic power became painfully obvious to all concerned. When in 1981 President Ronald Reagan fired the striking air-traffic controllers it suddenly became clear: without political power traditional labor unions were essentially dead. They were slowly replaced by the public service employees unions, by New Labor.

New Labor represents a new, transitional 'species' in social 'evolution'. It is still largely economically motivated, but it is politically organized under a politically motivated radical leadership. As a result, New Labor is no longer part of the 'working class' by any definition. New Labor is firmly embedded in the so-called middle classes, both in economic and political sense.

7.20 — The Middle Classes

According to Marxism the middle classes in a capitalist society were the groups below the capitalists (owners of capital) and above the exploited working classes (proletariat and peasantry). They were literally in the middle of social hierarchy.

In postwar America middle class came to mean white-collar workers. These were people who worked in offices and received monthly salaries as opposed to hourly wages. They were better educated, usually with college or university degrees. They typically made more money than factory workers — but they were still employed, they still worked for a living.

Marxists generally did not trust the middle classes. They considered them paid agents of the ruling classes who helped to exploit the working classes. They were also politically and culturally conservative. It didn't help that most European middle classes sided with the Nazis or the fascists before and during the Second World War.

This simplistic view of the middle classes was one of the biggest mistakes orthodox Marxists made; they didn't just ignore the complexity of the middle classes, they also underestimated their importance.

The terminology 'working class', 'middle class', 'bourgeoisie, 'ruling class, 'capitalism', 'capitalist', etc. are all Marxist in origin. Their widespread use and the lack of accepted alternative terminology illustrates how deeply embedded Marxism is in 'social science'. For the lack of commonly accepted alternatives these same terms are used in this book. This in no way endorses the validity of these Marxist concepts.

The middle classes are very large and growing fast. With the development of the service economy and the rise of information technology the middle classes became the dominant economic and social power. Today the middle classes control the most important element of the new economy: knowledge and knowhow. There is a very good reason why we call our economy "knowledge based".

Eventually, the New Left understood the political implications of all these changes and all this complexity. This was not an accident. The theorists and the activists of the New Left were right there when all these changes took place. They were teaching at the universities where the new middle class was born, where it was trained and educated. New Left theorists recognized the fundamental differences between the old and the new middle classes. This discovery gave them crucial advantages. They also realized that the middle classes were made up of significantly different groups.

The propaganda efforts of New Left politicians reflect the realization and acceptance of these facts. New Left campaign speeches almost never refer to the 'proletariat' anymore. They also use the word "worker" sparingly, usually in speeches delivered to blue collar audiences. Perversely, they also misuse the word "worker" to describe all government employees, presumably to deflect public animosity against government bureaucrats and their privileges. On the other hand, New Left campaign speeches frequently make claims to represent the interests of the "middle classes".

The infinitely diverse middle classes can be divided into three basic categories. One is the group working in newly emergent science based occupations. Another is made up of employees of the fast growing service economy. The last one consists of the old style professions.

Different techniques had to be used to exploit these three very different groups.

7.21 — Service Employees

The service economy employs vast numbers of people. Most of them are not really part of the middle class even if they think they are. To be middle class you have to have some education, some training that gives you the ability to perform specialized tasks. There are no clear definitions of middle class service employees. Fortunately, this is not necessary for our purposes here. A few hard and fast rules of thumb will suffice in order to identify this group.

To be middle class (service employee or otherwise) one should have some education, probably a community college degree or vocational training with a certificate. One should have a job that requires training, a job that could not be filled by hiring someone off the street and training him for a few days.

A good rule of thumb is that if you are a member of the SEIU (Service Employees International Union) you are probably not middle class.

Service employees are the least useful group of the middle classes for the purposes of the New Left. They are usually not motivated enough economically. If they were, they would try to improve their own economic situation rather than stay put and fight politically.

SEIU members mostly belong to the lower ranks of the working classes, often minority people harboring resentments. Many of them are just exploited by unscrupulous union bosses. The SEIU phenomenon should make an interesting study, but in the larger scheme of things they are irrelevant.

For these and other reasons we will ignore service employees, middle class or not. They only matter politically if they are ideologically motivated and become activists. Presently, they are largely inactive.

Service employees' support of political parties is split and soft. The majority of them are Democrats. The higher up we go on the social scale the more likely we'll find Republicans. Their political attitude, however, is generally passive and lukewarm.

7.22 — Techies

People in science and technology based occupations are definitely middle class.

Unfortunately, this does not provide us with a clear understanding of their political affiliations. Fortunately, New Leftists have the same problem: they don't really have a handle on this group of people.

Techies are usually very smart. They are also more resistant to ideological indoctrination practiced by the New Left at the universities. They are not totally immune to propaganda, but not nearly as vulnerable as students of social sciences or humanities. This is because the practice of real science requires the acceptance of objective truth. Such affirmation invalidates one of the main tenets of New Left ideology: conceptual and moral relativism.

Incidentally, these groups are on the forefront of both social and economic development. They are often self-employed or own small businesses. They have huge economic power and they can potentially change the structure of society. Frequently they become entrepreneurs and eventually capitalists. Many of them are foreign born.

Since they are not part of the New Left's present strategy we will largely ignore them, too. This does not mean, however, that they are not important in the larger scheme of things. They are and they will be much more so in the future.

7.23 — The Professional Classes

Theorists of the New Left made a momentous discovery soon after World War II. They recognized that they had wide ranging common interests with the traditional professional classes. They were smart enough to keep this discovery to themselves.

Up until this realization Marxist thinkers regarded professionals the same as policemen: paid helpers of the ruling classes. Marxist dogma stated that social position — which was based on economic interests — determined political views. They applied this belief to professionals too, even though many of them became Marxists early on for ideological reasons.

To casual observers this Marxist dogma seemed accurate. Professionals, by and large, were conservative, at least originally. Before and during both World Wars they mostly supported their governments against foreign enemies and domestic troublemakers just as the working classes did. In the 20th century, however, the economy and society have drastically changed. These changes had potentially devastating effects on the traditional professions.

Who are these professionals?

The common meaning of the term refers to highly educated people who work in a clearly defined field. Almost always a license is required to practice a profession. Professionals are well paid and they have a high social status.

Professions developed in the Middle Ages along with the bourgeoisie (industrial capitalists). Traditionally, — as commoners — capitalists and professionals were allies against the aristocracy and the clergy, the ruling classes of medieval societies. Once capitalism triumphed over medieval feudalism the bourgeoisie acquired most economic power. From this point on Marxism considered them and all their allies class enemies. They were on the opposite end of the newly emerging social scale from the proletariat.

How could these professional groups become potential allies of the New Left?

After the collapse of the Roman Empire and the dark ages that followed society developed very slowly. New classes emerged, partially along ethnic and tribal lines but also according to social function.

The soldiers and their leaders eventually became the nobility. They grabbed political power and they also owned most of the land.

Priests and monks became the clergy. They held spiritual power and the Catholic Church owned the remaining land.

The peasants, who worked the fields, stayed at the bottom of society. They had no power and they didn't own anything, not even their own labor (at least not entirely).

Over the centuries some of those who worked — especially in the newly re-emerging cities — acquired special skills. The most prominent of these were cathedral builders, weapon makers, merchants, sailors, artists, and so on. Since their skills were in great demand and they were not easy to replace they attained a certain amount of economic power. They guarded their knowledge jealously often passing it down through the generations. They employed other people. Eventually, they formed guilds to protect their interests.

These guilds controlled the practice and training of their professions, issued certificates of qualifications and licenses, protected their members from competition, regulated their prices, etc. They became very powerful in the cities of Europe. They usually worked under a charter issued by the king or prince. They paid taxes in exchange for their privileges. Often they governed their own cities, at least partially.

The industrial revolution spelled trouble for the guilds. New technologies made many of their skills irrelevant from one day to the next. The development of efficient production methods made them uncompetitive. Their carefully constructed system of rules became meaningless as they couldn't protect themselves against cheap, mass-produced products. Some of the guild members became capitalists themselves, the rest slid down the social scale and ended up as laborers.

This process was even more pronounced in America where the guilds didn't have deep roots to begin with. America was all about entrepreneurship, and capitalism was the engine destined to develop a new world order.

A few professions managed to take a stand and resist the overwhelming economic onslaught. These lucky few were not part of the emerging system of mass production. They were not producing things; they were providing services, specific but essential services.

Slowly but surely these surviving professions rebuilt their defenses against competition. The fast development of science helped them. More knowledge meant more complexity making their fields harder to invade. These professionals formed alliances and with the help of their new organizations they lobbied legislators and government officials for protection. Eventually, they became very powerful. Still, not all of them survived.

The most important of these professions were the lawyers and the doctors.

7.24 — Doctors and Healthcare

Doctors dominate the entire field of medicine. They feel entitled to be in control of health care.

The medical profession had humble beginnings. In antiquity most doctors were slaves. In the Middle Ages barbers and physicians were usually one and the same. Medical knowledge was woefully inadequate and through most of history doctors were far more likely to kill a patient than to cure him. Medical science only developed with the scientific and industrial revolution. Yet, many medieval universities did teach medicine as one of their four main subjects. (The other three were: arts, law and theology.)

As early as 1518 the Royal College of Physicians received a charter from the English King. The American Medical Association was established in 1847. Up until then 'doctors' operated in America like any other businessmen. They were judged only by the free market. Government licensing didn't appear until 1873, when the State of Texas established a licensing board. The first national examinations happened in 1915, less than a hundred years ago.

Since then, however, the medical profession grew in leaps and bounds.

Through much of their history American doctors had to wage war on two fronts. On one hand, they had to defend their specialty against capitalist intruders, who would turn medicine into a field of mass production and distribution. This was a very real danger; it had happened to many other sectors of the economy: agriculture, retail, pharmacies and pharmaceuticals, journalism, engineering, restaurants, shoemakers, tailors, and many others.

On the other hand, they had to defend their interests against government intrusion and meddling. Social reformers pressured doctors to participate in various welfare schemes. The federal government sued and convicted them for violating provisions of the Sherman Antitrust Act. Doctors fought against chiropractors, Medicare and HMO-s. They won some of these fights, but not all.

Nevertheless, today the medical profession is very well entrenched. Only licensed medical professionals are allowed to perform medical procedures. It is almost impossible for outsiders to establish a business or other organization to provide medical services. There are strict rules within the profession to regulate competition. Physicians have complicated and highly regulated relationships with each other, with registered nurses, hospitals, insurance companies, pharmaceutical companies, government agencies, medical schools, equipment manufacturers, and so on. Not to mention patients.

Health care spending consumes 16% of the Gross Domestic Product of the United States, the highest proportion of any developed country. Soon it will reach 20%. Medical costs play a significant role in more than half of personal bankruptcies. Yet, the results are not so positive. Life expectancy of Americans lag compared to other nations.

Clearly, something is wrong. Numerous efforts have been made to somehow reform our healthcare system. The latest of them is the 2010 healthcare reform signed into law by President Obama and now known as 'Obamacare'. All efforts to reform health care focused mainly on health insurance issues, on who pays for what and how much. Any promised savings would mostly come from supposed price controls and rationing of services by government agencies.

All reform efforts deal only with the demand side of health care. They are concerned with patients' needs and desires, how much they are willing and able to pay and who would finance the rest: employers, insurance companies or taxpayers. They propose to distribute health care based on the assumption that it is necessarily and chronically in short supply.

Nobody is talking about the supply side of health care. This is really astonishing if we consider the fact that health care is not a natural resource, it is simply a product. Moreover, the main component of this product is information, most of which is in the public domain (no longer under patent or copyright — with the exception of new drugs) and easily replicated. Much of this information is complex. Many other industries handle large quantities of complex information far more efficiently.

Consider the essence of medical treatment. It has two major elements, diagnosis and treatment. The process of diagnosis (finding out what is wrong) is purely about information. It involves asking the right questions, examining the relevant organs or tissues, testing body chemistry, evaluating x-rays, etc. All information collected needs to be analyzed, compared and verified. A significant part of this process is best done by computers.

What happens instead? When you visit the doctor's office you can make a few striking observations. The receptionist has a computer but the doctor doesn't. They make you fill out numerous forms, half of which are concerned with money and insurance. The rest is medical history that you have provided many times to various other doctors, but it is not accessible to your doctor since he has no computer. Even if he did he would have no access to your data. The information you just provided will not be computerized either, except the insurance related items. Furthermore, the doctor will only glance at the papers you carefully filled out. He will only ask a few questions and will barely listen to your answers. At the end he may give you a prescription for medication(s) or he will send you to a specialist. In rare cases you will receive an injection, undergo an operation or some other medical treatment.

You may or may not take the prescribed pills. Most likely you will get better (with or without the pills). If you are seriously ill, have cancer, heart condition or some rare disease that cannot readily be cured by drugs or fixed by routine surgery you are in big trouble. You will keep going to various doctors, get different treatments but the odds are against you.

What is wrong with this picture?

Nothing, according to the medical profession. Doctors would have you believe that medicine is just as much an art as a science. By that they mean that it is a sort of magic they alone can practice.

In reality, the most important ingredient of this process (information) is handled very inefficiently. Every doctor sees patients with the same problems all the time. He gives the same prescriptions. The problems he is not readily familiar with he passes on to somebody else. Even if you have a different problem, he is likely to see what he sees most of the time, and misdiagnose you. You may not find out about this until much later, if ever.

Every year almost 200,000 people die in American hospitals due to preventable medical errors. The numbers of non-lethal injuries caused by medical errors are truly staggering. Medical errors kill more Americans than alcohol, motor vehicle accidents, illegal drugs or guns. Far more people are killed by medical errors than homicide and suicide combined.

Is there an alternative?

Most certainly.

The health care monopoly of the medical profession must be broken. Doctors currently have a monopoly on diagnosing illness. The American Medical Association even copyrighted the lists — the very names — of diseases, treatments, procedures and their assigned code numbers used for processing insurance payments. Doctors have a monopoly on prescribing drugs. They have a monopoly on performing most medical procedures. They have more power over your own body, over your own health than you do. They also have restrictive licensing rules that limit the number of doctors.

All these monopolies must be abolished. This does not mean that anybody should be allowed to perform brain surgery. It does mean, however, that the medical field must be opened to other enterprises that are not necessarily run by doctors. Medical services must be provided based on strict scientific methods and practices. Hunches should never replace careful analysis. 'Art' should not masquerade as science.

The health care delivery system must also be reformed. The bottleneck deliberately built into the system must be removed. Presently, all medical care has to pass through the hands of physicians. This process is inefficient, slow, expensive and often counterproductive. This medieval arrangement serves the medical profession well, but it is against the interests of patients and society.

Medical education must also be reformed. The knowledge required to be a good doctor is far too much for anyone to know. Yet, medical students are required to memorize reams of information most of which they will never use, they barely understand and will soon forget. Medical schools serve as gatekeepers to restrict entry to the profession. They must be modernized, reorganized and simplified. Doctors should learn what they need to know, not more and not less.

Consider what food production and distribution would be like if they were organized the same way as our health care system is. Restaurants could be operated only by licensed nutritionists. Waiters and busboys would be required to undergo rigorous training and examinations. Ingredients would be tightly controlled. Everything would be recorded in great detail. Customers would have to eat what they are told and how much they are allotted. There would be procedures manuals instead of recipes. We would soon starve to death. The Pentagon's 26 page recipe for brownies is well worth studying.

None of this means that doctors should be thrown out to the streets. We will need good physicians in the future, too.

They will still be highly skilled and well paid. But the monopoly must be broken so the country (and the patients) can survive.

Up till now no competition was able to challenge the monopoly of the medical profession, not in the United States, nor abroad. This is because all developed countries operate essentially under the same system. The demand side is often organized differently in other countries resulting in alternative insurance schemes and regulations. The supply side, the production and delivery of health care, however, is very much the same in all developed countries.

This arrangement may not last for long. It is entirely feasible for China, Japan or some other country to develop an alternative method. Medical tourism is already a reality. We should reform our own system before it is destroyed by others. Many other industries have suffered the same fate. Doctors, of course, are worried about these possibilities. They don't want to end up like the pharmacists did. They don't want to end up working for Walgreens, Walmart or Rite Aid. They should be worried. They may end up as the auto workers instead.

The present system is unfair and unsustainable.

What does any of this have to do with the New Left, minorities and Bolshevism?

Quite a lot, actually. All monopolies require political power to sustain them; some more than others. The medical monopoly is highly dependent on political power, on government regulations. The medical profession lobbies both political parties. They are, however, natural allies with the Democrats, with the Left. This is because their monopolistic needs require government protection, and restrictions imposed on the competition. Any viable competition would be based on economic power and by definition is outside the medical profession. The Left (both old and new) lives and breathes through political power and government regulation.

Not all doctors are Democrats, of course. But the profession as a whole is definitely allied with the Left, especially the New Left. The American Medical Association has to navigate treacherous waters, but they know who their ultimate allies are.

Furthermore, doctors represent only a small fraction of people who are employed in the health care industry. There are many others: nurses, aids, hospital workers, dentists, psychiatrists, chiropractors, physical therapists, various medical service providers, receptionists and administrators, care givers of all sorts, and so on. Overall, the health care field represents one-sixth of the US economy with the corresponding workforce and economic power.

Interestingly, Obamacare itself can be interpreted as an all-out attack on the medical profession and medical professionals. The entire legislation is actually an ideologically motivated extension of government power. While it seemingly leaves the medical monopoly intact it imposes a great degree of direct and indirect government control over it. Carried to its logical conclusion this effort will transfer the cherished medical monopoly into government hands. By taking control of the distribution and reimbursement side of health care the government is attempting to establish near total control of the entire system. For all practical purposes most physicians would become subordinates of government regulators and bureaucrats. Not quite employees yet, but subservient to direct government power, political power. Introduction of the much promoted 'public option' will complete the government takeover.

For many years government guidelines determined which treatments (HCPCS codes) were appropriate for which diagnoses (ICD-9 codes). More and more patients along with their doctors fall under these increasingly stringent rules. Soon, they all will be subjected to them.

Many doctors were against Obamacare, but their very own professional organization, the American Medical

Association supported it. Political power triumphed. The New Left won another battle. Whether the medical profession will benefit from it or not remains to be seen.

Other developed countries have different health care systems. Most of them are similar to ours, more or less along the described path of development. Their problems and experiences deserve insightful analysis in light of the issues discussed here.

7.25 — Lawyers and the Legal System

Lawyers are worse than doctors. Much worse.

This seemingly arrogant statement may sound contemptuous but it is essentially true. How so?

Doctors sometimes suggest unnecessary medical procedures to their patients. They are not alone in this regard. Car mechanics do the same kind of thing. Customers are routinely sold products and services they don't really need or want. Of course, unnecessarily changing the timing belt in your Chevy is not the same as getting an unnecessary triple bypass. Another problem is the advisory relationship. Doctors and other professionals are not supposed to be salesmen; they act as trusted advisors, supposedly serving their patients' best interests. Still, doctors and car mechanics mostly deal with real problems that exist in objective reality.

Lawyers, on the other hand, create many of the problems themselves: not fake, make-believe problems, but real ones. They create problems where no problems existed before and they do it on a large scale. They do this by concocting unnecessary, vague and harmful laws, writing convoluted contracts with uncertain and contradictory meaning, making irrational and outrageous claims and arguments, bringing unfair and unreasonable judgments, and so on. Their propensity to do mischief has been well documented through the centuries. The medical equivalent of this strategy would be to create epidemics in order to drum up business.

Physicians deal with natural problems.

Lawyers deal with laws created by lawyers.

Most lawyers, of course, are not legislators, and thus they don't write laws. Most legislators, on the other hand, are lawyers, and they do write lots of laws, many (if not most) of them bad.

None of this means that without lawyers there would be no problems. There would still be disagreements to deal with. Thus, society needs laws and even lawyers. Unfortunately, many of the laws we have are not designed to solve our problems. To a large extent they are designed to benefit the lawyers and their political allies.

Throughout history laws were made for the benefit of the powerful. Making laws did involve lawyers but they were mostly hired hands doing the dirty work. They were involved mainly to make sure the law would work, like engineers who built machines or architects who built cathedrals. They did benefit from the process but it was primarily not designed for them.

Lawyers originally were orators (BS artists), people with talent for public speaking, sometimes trained in the art of rhetoric. The law itself developed as a function of complexity. As political entities, cities, states and empires grew, governing them became more and more difficult and complex. Rules were made to facilitate the functioning of government. These rules had to make sense, they had to work together and they had to be enforced. Rules that withstood time were kept; they were written down and became law.

Generally speaking, the more sophisticated, the more complex and the more long-lasting a society was, the more laws it had. Empires were especially good at making laws. The Roman Empire and the Catholic Church both created lots of complex laws. As a result lawyers flourished under their reigns.

On the other hand, both laws and lawyers disappeared during the Dark Ages. Both the French and the Russian (Bolshevik) revolutions decimated the ranks of lawyers, who were intimately connected with the previous regimes. Soon thereafter new lawyers were needed to keep the government machinery functioning and the guillotines and firing squads fully utilized.

Thus, lawyers seem to be a necessary evil.

But how necessary? And how evil?

Picture this: you and your spouse are newly married. You move into a new house. Every time something happens you have to decide what to do about it. As soon as you make the decision you write up a rule for future reference and post it on the wall. Your spouse does the same, and so do your parents, your in-laws, your children and other relatives. How long do you think this can go on before your life becomes unbearable?

In 2008 alone the *Federal Register* published 79,435 pages. In 1958 this number was 10,579. Since 1988 it was never less than 50,000 pages. The 2009 edition of the *Code of Federal Regulations* contained 163,333 pages in 226 volumes. Add to these state laws, municipal codes and judicial precedents and you have a law library. A pretty big one.

Many laws are vague or contradictory. If all laws were followed the country would come to a standstill. Somewhat surprisingly, however, most of our laws are neither followed, nor enforced. How could that be? Why would they make laws if they don't expect them to be observed?

Think of these laws as weapons or ammunition. They are made to provide the government, politicians, their allies and lawyers with power. They are there to be used if and when they are needed and they are there to be a threat. Like most weapons they are rarely used. Their very existence is enough. Laws are very effective weapons. But let us not kid ourselves, when they need them they use them, unhesitatingly. Our lives, our businesses and our futures are booby trapped.

One would think that a well-developed, mature and free country should have a stable legal system. At some point there are sufficient numbers of well-crafted laws on the books. After that new laws should only be made when the need arises, when things change enough to require new rules. In reality, however, legislation is a growth industry and its growth is accelerating. We have long ago passed the natural balance when we had just the right number of laws.

Moreover, the law is invading new fields all the time. Hardly any aspect of life remains untouched by laws and lawyers. One of the newest and most troubling example is the intrusion of lawyers into foreign policy and war fighting. Lawyers increasingly interfere with command decisions of military officers on the battlefield. Double guessing military decisions became commonplace.

What does this have to do with the New Left and *Minority Bolshevism*?

For one thing, lawyers (just like doctors) are members of a minority directly benefiting from all these arrangements. In return they provide the holders of political power with weapons against their main rival, economic power. Remember, the strategy of Bolshevism is to take control of political power and use it against all other kinds of power, especially economic power. Lawyers are a big part of this struggle. They provide the most effective weapons.

Lawyers also invade and occupy the territories of other groups of the coalition built by the New Left. There are laws and lawyers in the healthcare sector, in education, in finance, in corporations, in all of the economy, in the media, in Hollywood and in the government itself, including the military. The groups under attack resent these intrusions but there is very little they can do. Lawyers act like an armed gang serving their own interests along those of the New Left. They are the *praetorian guard* of the New Left.

Some of these lawyers are far more dangerous and destructive than ordinary attorneys who sell their services to the general population. As a result, most people instinctively dislike lawyers in general even though they like their own attorneys. This is also true for other professions to a lesser extent, with the exception of government professionals, who are universally detested. Lawyers are usually not bad people as individuals. They just happen to be members of a profession that often behaves like a parasite.

There are many lawyers who work for big businesses. They are not necessarily associated with the New Left, nor particularly sympathetic to it. They serve businesses that command enormous economic power, and are often just as ruthless as their rivals, the holders of vast political power. Even right-wing lawyers, however, benefit from the New Left's policies of promoting legal malignancy. The tidal wave of complex and intrusive legislation raises the boats of all lawyers.

Many big businesses are inextricably intertwined with political power. They are often ideologically neutral; they deal with whomever is in power. Lawyers are always involved in these deals and the taxpayers usually end up paying for them.

During the last few decades the rule of law has been seriously distorted. This can easily be felt but it's hard to explain and almost impossible to pinpoint or prove. Here are just a few examples:

Fully half of the Bill of Rights (Amendments 4-8) were designed to safeguard our liberty by regulating and limiting legal processes used by the government. This gave rise to the theory that legal procedures were the most important guarantors of our lives and liberty. Procedural rules, however, multiplied to the point that no mortal can possibly understand them. You definitely need a lawyer to navigate them. Whether you are guilty or innocent are not nearly as important as the motions filed by the participating attorneys.

Clearly, the Founding Fathers established these rules to make sure the innocents are protected and the guilty are punished; not the other way around. Yet, under the direction from the New Left, these safeguards were turned inside out and upside down. For example, actual evidence of guilt is routinely excluded in criminal trials based on an ever expanding list of requirements regulating police procedures. 'Getting off on a technicality' became a common-place occurrence. These 'technicalities' are often nothing more than legal landmines. Members of protected minorities often enjoy privileges that affect the outcomes of legal cases, both criminal and civil.

Getting sued is one of the worst nightmares anyone can have. Whether it is divorce, a car accident, contractual dispute, customer complaint, employee grievance or bankruptcy, a lawsuit can ruin your life.

Not all lawsuits are created equal. Some are far more insidious and dangerous than others. Claims of damages (tort law) are some of the most harmful and troublesome lawsuits one can be subjected to. The objective versions of these claims (accidents, injuries) are bad enough. Claims of discrimination (racial, ethnic, religious, gender, sexual orientation, age, disability), harassment, product liability, wrongful termination, unfair competition, environmental violations and malpractice (Public Interest Law) can often mean the end of one's career, losing one's business, bankruptcy or worse. On the other side of the issue, tort claims are a very lucrative business for plaintiffs' lawyers. Not surprisingly, the tort bar is one of the biggest contributors to the Democratic Party. In exchange for their political contributions all attempts of legal reform are killed in the various legislative bodies.

Many of the laws governing these non-monetary, subjective injury disputes are intentionally vague. Courts often pass wildly different judgments in such cases.

Frequently such claims are used as weapons against political opponents. Both the laws and the courts generally favor left-wing positions in these matters. Entire government agencies staffed by hundreds of lawyers are set up to advocate and enforce predominantly leftist points of view.

The economic impact of these legal maneuvers is immense. The damages awarded by courts are only a small part of the overall costs. Defensive behavior and risk avoidance suppress economic activity immeasurable ways.

Unfortunately, there is no easy fix to this problem. Partial reforms — such as the much touted tort reform — would solve some problems but only at the expense of delaying other equally important reforms. Only a complete overhaul of the legal system would provide an acceptable solution. This, however, would require massive amounts of political will and power and the willing cooperation of the legal profession. The odds are very much in favor of the lawyers and their political allies against ordinary law abiding citizens.

7.26 — Education Professionals

As we have seen the New Left strategy of the "long march through the institutions" selected higher education as one of its primary targets. The New Left first infiltrated the social science departments of universities. Soon after that they invaded teachers' colleges. This was followed by a frontal attack on community colleges, the humanities and finally law schools.

Students of other fields (science, engineering, medicine, etc.) were also subjected to these indoctrination efforts. All courses that fell under the domain of the directly targeted fields advanced leftist propaganda. There were hardly any fields of study and hardly any students unaffected. Even religious institutions were attacked, often successfully.

Newly minted teachers with fully charged leftist views had spread out to primary and secondary education. As a result, several generations of schoolchildren were educated according to left-wing principles and absorbed New Left values. From kindergarten to post-doctoral studies leftist thinking dominates our education system.

The original invasion of higher education was carried out by seducing the intellectuals. This was not hard considering that intellectuals were always attracted to political power and resented economic power. College professors always looked down on businessmen and they found it very disturbing that these 'inferior' and 'uncultured' people often made much more money than they did. Intellectuals also resented the fact that businessmen were their own masters who didn't have to constantly justify their existence and their worth to bosses.

The New Left used a different strategy to invade primary and secondary education. They utilized long-standing allies and established methods to achieve their goals. Their primary allies were the teachers' unions, some of the oldest labor organizations in America. Under the guise of union representation agents of the New Left gradually took control of these unions. They capitalized on traditional concerns and valid complaints of teachers, such as wages, working hours and conditions. Once they were in leadership positions they radically expanded their ideological and political dominance.

To be sure, teachers' unions (as most labor unions) always preferred left-wing ideology. This is simply because labor is traditionally in conflict with economic power, with capital and management. This conflict is natural and labor unions play a legitimate role in the economy. The problem arises when labor's conflict with capital becomes a struggle against capitalism itself. Bolshevism always tried to use labor unions as a force in its struggle to destroy capitalism. Only the methods changed when the New Left took over.

Under the control of the New Left the NEA (National Education Association) and the AFT (American Federation of Teachers) greatly expanded the unions' ideological and political efforts. They openly and aggressively promoted political correctness, gay rights, radical feminism, racial agendas, environmentalism, and all sorts of political programs under the slogans of social justice and progressivism. They not only supported all these leftist causes; they also tried to make them part of the official school curriculum. They largely succeeded.

While invading education from the inside (via the unions) the New Left also attacked from the outside. Exploiting widespread and often justified resentments against racial segregation, they launched an attack on the entire school system of the United States. They set out to remake the way school districts were organized. First came the 1954 unanimous Supreme Court decision (Brown v. Board of Education) abolishing racial segregation laws. Ten years later the Civil Rights Act outlawed racial segregation practices. A few years after that various federal courts issued a series of decisions redrawing school district boundaries and ordering forced busing of schoolchildren, supposedly to achieve actual racial desegregation. While this arguably admirable goal remained largely elusive the court decisions did have other far reaching effects. They have torn apart well-established school districts and effectively ended local community control over schools.

Control of the schools passed into the hands of bureaucrats and activists.

In the name of fighting racism federal and state governments sent countless government functionaries to schools and school districts. Many school districts became huge unwieldy institutions. Parents lost contact with teachers, principals and other administrators. All administrative personnel became members of the teachers' unions. New, complex rules proliferated.

Soon the curriculum also began to change. To equalize test scores many subjects were dumbed down. The teachers' unions declared war on merit pay and resisted all efforts of firing inept teachers. In a single generation the quality of elementary and high school education went from excellent to dreadful. At the same time the cost of education skyrocketed.

All parents who could afford to do so took their children out of public schools. Some of the rest decided to fight the system trying to get merit pay, charter schools, school vouchers, etc. The education establishment resisted all reform efforts.

Today a large proportion of students graduate from high school without the necessary skills to survive in an increasingly competitive economy. Many of them can barely read and write, they hardly know any math, but they are fully trained in leftist ideology. Many of them go on to study in community colleges. Many of these institutions supply the nation with legions of graduates ready to work in the service economy. They will work in retail, in offices, in government agencies, in marketing, in customer service and so on. The ideologically motivated ones will go into social work and education.

Meanwhile, more than half of all students accepted to science related fields in our best universities are foreigners. They come from countries where the education system wasn't destroyed yet. They will become scientists, computer programmers, financiers, engineers, weapon designers, bankers and entrepreneurs.

The problems of our health care and education systems have important similarities. Both of them are controlled by a well-entrenched and legally protected professional group. Healthcare is controlled by doctors; education is controlled by professors. Both fields are protected from outside competition. Doctors have medical licensing; universities and professors have accreditation and tenure.

Universities have to be accredited in order to function. Accreditation gives the right to an education institution to issue a university degree. Without this right the university cannot exist. Universities are accredited by regional associations of member universities. This peer review process is supposed to ensure the continued high quality of university education. It also makes outside competition next to impossible.

This rigid, guild-type, cartel-like, restrictive arrangement keeps higher education very expensive by limiting the supply. It also ensures that professors remain a well paid, well protected and exclusive group of professionals. This is clearly good for the professors but not so good for the students or the taxpayers.

University accreditation has another troublesome side effect. Because of these restrictions the only practical way to get accreditation is to buy an existing university that already has one. As a result, for-profit organizations buy financially failing but accredited institutions. These newly reorganized for-profit universities admit students regardless of qualifications. At the end thousands upon thousands of graduates enter the workforce with valid but largely useless diplomas. They also owe large amounts of student loans to be paid back later.

The recent rise of for-profit universities is similar to the spread of gambling establishments on Native American Reservations. Both were based on the exploitation of a legal loophole and both had far-reaching economic and social consequences.

Interestingly, hospitals have their own accreditation requirements.

Tenure is another guild-like protection for the benefit of professors. It is usually awarded by a committee of other tenured professors of the same institution. It provides lifetime job security. Its primary justification is the guarantee of academic freedom. In reality, it is mostly just a self-serving protection against outside competition.

In social and political science, economics, journalism and humanities departments of many universities leftist professors represent an overwhelming majority. They use tenure as a shield to defend themselves against any and all criticism. They are essentially untouchable. They have guaranteed rights to indoctrinate future generations of students as they see fit.

Our education system has another major structural problem, very similar to what we have seen in the health care system. It affects all levels of education, although not equally.

Education is not a natural resource. It is a product. The essence of education (just like the essence of health care) is information. Most of this information is in the public domain. In addition, the fair-use doctrine of US copyright law specifically allows the teaching of copyrighted works. Thus, the information itself which is being thought is essentially freely available. Yet, education is very expensive. Why is that?

Just like in health care, there is a built-in bottleneck in the distribution of education. All information delivered by our education system must pass through the hands of teachers. We teach our kids essentially the same way as they were thought in the Stone Age. Our kids sit around a room and a teacher tells them what the education establishment thinks they should learn. Any technology used is also under the control of the teacher. The textbooks that contain all the public domain information are themselves copyrighted. In effect the packaging that contains the freely available information is very expensive. Textbooks and other classroom materials are produced under cartel-like conditions and restrictions. There is even an effort trying to make the resale of used textbooks illegal based on copyright grounds.

Testing of students has similar problems. Most tests used are copyrighted. They must be administered and evaluated by teachers.

Trigonometry was developed by ancient Greek mathematicians. Calculus was invented by Newton. Yet, they are sold today in copyrighted packaging to students who are obligated to buy them for a fixed price. If they manage to learn them they are required to take copyrighted tests administered by licensed professionals. They have to take these tests again and again as they advance through the labyrinth of the school system. We all pay dearly over and over for knowledge freely available outside this monopolized information delivery system. If food distribution was priced according to the same principles we would die of hunger.

None of this means that we should get rid of teachers, professors, schools or universities. It does mean, however, that our education system must be drastically reformed. The education monopoly must be broken up. Education must be opened up to outside competition. Testing should be done by organizations independent of schools. Businesses, who will hire the new graduates, should have input into the curriculum and the tests. Schools should teach knowledge that is useful in the real world, not what is useful for the schools.

Degrees and diplomas should be issued by independent testing institutions, not the schools. Some of these tests and testing institutions already exist. The CPA exam (for accountants), the bar exam (for attorneys) and other professional examinations (architects, structural engineers, etc.) are examples of such testing. Anybody should be eligible to take these exams regardless how they acquired the knowledge. There should be no mandatory course requirements.

Schools and teachers should be judged according to the test results of their students. They should be paid based on supply and demand. All school accreditation should be abolished. Reputable private enterprises should be able to open and operate schools. All children of citizens and resident aliens should get a minimum amount of vouchers from the government. They could use these vouchers to buy education services from whomever they want. Businesses or non-profit institutions would have to post performance guarantees in order to be able to cash these vouchers. They could get these guarantees by buying insurance or posting a bond.

Students who perform well on standardized tests should get more vouchers from the government so they could continue their education. State and local governments would be allowed to operate schools and universities as before, but without the monopoly. Foreign students could buy vouchers. Individual teachers could go to business for themselves. They could establish their own schools, alone or in cooperation with other teachers. Teacher credentialing should not be mandatory.

All student, teacher and school records should be available to the public from a central source. No copyrighted textbook would be required for any course. Copyrighting textbooks would be allowed but no captive market should be provided for them.

These are just a few ideas for reform. Reorganizing our education system is a very big deal. It would take sober analysis and careful implementation to make it work. But it is entirely possible to carry out such major reforms, indeed it must be done. The education monopoly must be terminated.

7.27 — Government Professionals

The definition of government professionals is not as clear cut as the definition of legal, medical or education professionals. Indeed, many lawyers, doctors and teachers are government employees themselves. There are millions of other government employees (such as soldiers) who also don't fall into this category. So what are we talking about?

The term *government professional* denotes the group of people who make the machinery of government work. Not all government employees are professionals (janitors, cafeteria workers, etc.) and not all professionals working for the government (doctors, teachers, engineers, etc.) are government professionals. This is not necessarily a precise distinction, nor is it critical. It is important, however, for understanding government professionals' unique role within the government.

Traditionally, government professionals were members of the civil service in charge of public administration. Because of complexity every country needs people with specialized expertise to ensure the smooth functioning of its government. Ancient empires (Rome, China) developed complex bureaucracies for this purpose thousands of years ago.

To ensure stability these bureaucracies needed to be insulated from the constant political struggle for power. Rulers who recognized this need granted various protections to their civil service. Bureaucrats in turn remained loyal but politically neutral servants of the state. Modern democracies enshrined these protections in law. Detailed rules were adopted to govern every aspect of civil service, including job and income protection, pensions, authority, dispute resolution and so on.

These privileges along with government sanctioned authority made bureaucrats very powerful. They administered laws, issued permits, collected taxes, imposed fines and penalties, levied fees and made all sorts of decisions directly affecting the lives of people. Not surprisingly, civil servants were never very popular.

Their power often enabled government bureaucrats to take advantage of ordinary citizens. Corruption is as old as government and it is still widespread today.

In the United States civil service was established after the Civil War. Several laws were passed over the years regulating all aspects of civil service. Starting in 1939 civil servants were not permitted to take part in political activities. Since they enjoyed civil service protections they were not eligible to unionize.

All that changed with a stroke of a pen on January 17, 1962. On that day President John F. Kennedy signed

Executive Order 10988 granting federal employees the right to unionize for the first time in history. This quickly led to the unionization of other government employees at the state, county and municipal levels. Federal government employees' right to unionize was codified into law by the Civil Service Reform Act of 1978 signed into law by President Carter. Today there are 79 unions with "exclusive recognition with departments and agencies of the Executive Branch of the Federal Government", plus seven more Postal Service unions.

With this new arrangement the balance of power significantly shifted in favor of government employees. These changes ushered in a relentless expansion of public employees' power. This affected everything: their salaries, their benefits, their work rules and their attitudes. As a result, the growth of the public sector itself became unstoppable.

JFK, of course, was a creature of the Left. He knew what he was doing. The same way FDR permanently bound several groups to the Democratic Party (including labor unions and blacks), JFK secured the votes of another group: government employees. Kennedy achieved an additional goal; he successfully politicized a potentially very powerful force.

Union organizers were by definition left-wing. Civil servants had an intrinsic interest to unionize. They had nothing to lose and everything to gain. More money, more security, more power. They took advantage of the gift President Kennedy offered them. They got the message and they lived up to their side of the bargain. They became servants of the Left.

The so-called *Great Society* programs introduced by Kennedy's successor Lyndon B. Johnson generated a further huge growth in government. For every conceivable social or economic problem it provided the same answer: government help. New agencies proliferated as government programs multiplied. Graduates of the newly reformed education system eagerly joined these efforts. They all became members of public sector unions. They knew what they were supposed to do. Most of them were true believers. The New Left has conquered government.

This power shift proved to be permanent. Since Executive Order 10988 was signed no one was able to resist the power of public sector unions. Not even the Reagan Revolution could push back these groups dominated by leftist ideology and protected by law. Their influence steadily increases as their numbers constantly grow.

Government employee unions and their members overwhelmingly support the Democratic Party. They unhesitatingly use government power to further leftist agendas. Most of them believe that they are doing good. Of course, they never forget to take care of their own interests as well.

7.28 — Financial Professionals

Financial professionals are not ideologically motivated. They care about one thing and one thing only: money.

Who are these much maligned individuals?

Financial professionals handle other people's money (OPM). There are many varieties of them: bankers, brokers, investment advisors, insurance agents, asset allocators, traders, dealers, underwriters, speculators, hedge fund managers and others.

The OPM distinction is very important. We should never mistake financial professionals for capitalists. Having said that, we have to realize that sometimes even real capitalists (bona-fide entrepreneurs) investing their own money can endanger capitalism, the very system that produces all goods and services we need to survive. How could that be?

It has to do with capital markets, the best known of which is the stock market. The stock market has a unique property. It can create money out of nothing. This ability is not very well understood even though it is based on a simple principle. It is the same principle that capitalism itself is based on. It is simply this: properly done, capitalist enterprise can produce more value than was originally contributed to it. The output is more than the total input. We end up with more than we started with. This phenomenon is commonly referred to as *surplus value*. Most of our current economic problems originate from not properly understanding the nature of *surplus value*.

Marx believed that all surplus value was simply stolen from labor, extorted from workers. His theory was based on the assumption that capitalist production is a zero sum game. In such a game every gain is matched by an equal loss somewhere else in the system. Therefore, profit must come from exploitation. To complicate things, profits sometimes do come from exploitation, but in a capitalist system this is neither necessary nor typical. In fact, the less exploitation is used, the less it is needed, the more viable an enterprise is. This is precisely why capitalism won against feudalism, why the Union won against the Confederacy and why the West won the Cold War.

Capital markets, especially the stock market, operate on the same principle. It is not necessary for someone to lose in order for someone else to gain. Both the buyer and the seller of a stock could make a profit.

Conversely, it is also possible for both the buyer and the seller of a stock to suffer a loss. Stock market profits are generated from price increases, and stock market losses are caused by price declines. This is the flipside of the stock market's magic: it can also make money disappear into nothing.

Financial professionals (handling other people's money) can profit both from price increases and from price declines. This is because **they** are usually part of a zero sum game. Any fee or commission they make is someone else's loss. When this someone else is making a profit on the (non-zero sum game) stock market, this loss is just an inconsequential transaction cost.

All of this is pretty confusing for most people, including most financial professionals. All they know and all they care about is their commissions, their fees, their share of the profits. Where those profits come from, how they are generated is not important for most of them.

The surplus value generated by capitalist enterprises is reflected in increased prices of stocks. Thus, the profits everyone shares in are ultimately produced by these capitalist enterprises, capitalism itself. Unfortunately, surplus value is not the only factor affecting stock prices. Supply and demand for the stocks themselves influence the stock market greatly. These factors cannot be separated or even measured.

There is an optimal level of capital market activity. At any given moment there is also an optimal allocation of capital. As circumstances change capital needs to move from one company to another, from one sector to another. Too much friction slows down this process causing inefficiency. Too much (or too fast) capital movement is also counterproductive. Unfortunately, there is no objective way to decide what the optimal price level is or what the optimal capital movements should be. It seems reasonably certain, however, that during the last few decades at least, there was much too much of both.

Financial professionals have a vested interest both in rising stock prices and in increasing trading volume. This is no different from the interests of other professionals. Doctors benefit from diseases (real or imagined) and lawyers benefit from lawsuits (necessary or not). When stock prices rise the volume of trading also increases. This in turn generates an increase in the number of financial professionals. More financial professionals encourage yet more trading which in turn generates further price increases. There is a very strong feedback effect in financial markets.

The stock market is only one of many financial markets. There are markets for bonds (government, corporate, municipal, foreign), for commodities (raw materials, oil, gold), for services (insurance, banking, credit), for currencies (dollar, euro, yen), for futures (commodities, stock indices) and for other more exotic 'financial products' (options, derivatives). Some of these markets are based on surplus value creation, but most of them are zero sum games. For example, producing commodities may generate surplus value, but trading commodities is generally a zero sum game.

Not all financial instruments are well suited for trading. Unfortunately, this did not prevent highly trained and very creative financial professionals to devise ways to trade them anyway. Financial 'engineers' designed countless new financial instruments and built markets where they could be traded.

This is the point where financial professionals, the government and *Minority Bolshevism* intersect.

Financial markets are regulated by government. This has been a fact of life for a long time. Furthermore, they are getting progressively more regulated. Partly this is due to past mistakes. Every time there is a major setback in the financial markets government invariably intervenes and imposes new regulations. Even so-called deregulation is nothing more than a set of new rules, different regulations. Government "never lets a crisis go to waste" in order to expand its own power.

Financial institutions themselves are also highly regulated. Government agencies established for this very purpose supervise all aspects of financial institutions. Their books are open to government inspectors and they are constantly audited. Government overseers, however, often don't understand what they are seeing. Unfortunately, the financial institutions themselves don't always know what they are doing either.

Financial institutions and financial professionals are always on the lookout for new trading opportunities. The development of sophisticated computers created many new possibilities. Technological innovation made trading extremely fast and relatively cheap. As more and more people got involved the demand for tradable financial instruments increased markedly. This, in turn, caused prices to rise. The golden age of capital markets, investment banking and trading has arrived.

Financial 'engineers' soon realized that they could easily turn any contract, any financial relationship into a tradable financial instrument. Securitization was born. Credit card receivables, mortgages, complicated multi-party swap agreements all became standardized securities. Soon anyone could bet on any measurable price movement of just about anything.

Every new financial instrument was categorized into a previously existing group regulated by a dedicated government agency. Often these classifications didn't quite fit. Many new securities were significantly different from anything that existed before. Government regulators had trouble understanding these new securities. This was understandable considering that many of them were described in prospectuses hundreds of pages long written in dense legal language. The financial professionals themselves never really read these documents either. They figured the market would tell them everything they needed to know. If somebody bought these instruments it was good enough for the pros. Everyone involved believed that someone else made sure these instruments were safe.

Government regulation was clearly losing ground. At the height of the stock market mania leading investment bankers decided to make a clean sweep. They lobbied Congress for major changes. They came to view government regulation as an inefficient, outdated and unnecessary burden on the financial services industry.

Their intensive lobbying effort paid off. Congress passed the Commodity Futures Modernization Act of 2000 (CFMA). The House of Representatives voted for it 292-60 and the Senate passed it with unanimous consent. In the House 51 republicans and 9 democrats voted against the bill. President Clinton signed it into law on December 21, 2000.

This misleadingly titled 262-page law had far reaching consequences. It removed several newly created financial instruments from any meaningful regulation. One of them (energy related bilateral swap agreements) became known as the "Enron Loophole". Another exemption was for *credit default swaps* whose proliferation facilitated the great expansion of subprime mortgages. Eventually, the trillions of dollars worth of bets made under the provisions of this law crushed the US real estate market and ushered in the biggest economic downturn since the Great Depression.

Most of this law (CFMA) is still in effect. Numerous other lesser known laws were passed with similar results.

Why would Congress enact such laws? Didn't they see the dangers?

Not really. As usual, most of them didn't bother to read the proposed legislation. But even if they did, they wouldn't have understood it. Furthermore, the government itself was hooked on the money that was being made on Wall Street. All these sophisticated transactions generated jobs, created tax revenues and increased prosperity. Fees, commissions and trading profits were all included in the GDP. They were also taxed.

Government has an incestuous relationship with financial institutions and financial professionals. The ability of creating money from nothing is irresistible. Of course, this newly created money is not free. It comes with a high price: increased risk.

By the way, there is another financial institution that can create money out of nothing: the central bank. However, the money issued by the Federal Reserve Bank is not free either. Too much money printed comes (literally) with a high price: inflation.

Well-functioning financial markets and financial institutions are essential for the economy. If they get out of control, however, they can damage or even destroy the economy. The government, financial professionals and large corporations directly benefit from well-functioning financial markets. Small business owners and workers also benefit, but only indirectly. They benefit from being part of a capitalist economy. When things go wrong they have nothing to defend themselves with against a financial meltdown, a stock market crash, inflation, recession and so on. For this reason small business owners are generally distrustful of Wall Street, the Federal Reserve and the Government itself.

Financial professionals have an alliance, an unwritten agreement with big government. They usually support both political parties, but often seem to prefer Democrats. Why? You would think that rich bankers and Wall Street types would tend to side with Republicans, who are usually considered favoring the rich. They often don't.

The real problem is the mixing of political and economic power. Not all financial relationships are suitable for trading and political power should definitely not be traded. But very often it is traded and this makes the financial profession an ally of the government. As we have seen, the machinery of government is largely controlled by the Left. Consequently, the financial profession is objectively allied with the Left, based on their mutual interests. One of the results of this alliance is that the financial sector is much bigger than necessary. There are far too many financial professionals.

Another result is the excessively high price level of stocks and other financial instruments. We tend to think that when food is cheap it is a good thing, but when stocks or real estate are expensive it is even better. In reality, everything has an appropriate price, even if we don't know what that is. When prices of stocks, currencies or real estate are overly high trouble lies ahead. This is especially true if we bought them with borrowed money. Similarly, it is neither good nor healthy when interest rates are near zero.

Financial professionals are not bad people. They are just like doctors and lawyers: we need them, the economy needs them. They serve a vital function. There are just far too many of them with far too much power.

When mishandling other people's money (OPM) causes trouble it often becomes an SEP (someone else's problem). Your problem. Our problem.

7.29 — Other Interest Groups

There are many other groups allied with the Left based on economic self interests. Some of them are organized, some are not so much. Sometimes, but not always, they also have an ideological motivation.

Traditional labor unions have a long standing relationship with the Left and with the Democratic Party. Likewise, recipients of government benefits or aid often prefer the more generous Left. This includes Social Security recipients, people on welfare or disability, students with subsidized tuition, and so on.

People operating businesses that receive government subsidies have a vested interest to keep that money flowing. Same with government contractors. Farm subsidies (including ethanol) amount to billions of dollars every year. They are amongst the oldest government assistance programs and they enjoy bipartisan support. Green technologies, solar power, electric cars and others are favorites of the New Left.

Naturally, right-wing politicians also have supporters, both ideologically and economically motivated.

While every vote counts, these groups are simply too small to make a strategic difference.

7.30 — Minority Bolshevism

The New Left coalition is essentially complete.

It contains two major factions. Each faction consists of several groups.

The activist faction includes all ideologically motivated groups. The objectives of all these groups are primarily political or ideological. Nevertheless, they are not above extorting material benefits for themselves and for their leaders. They all accept the ideologies of all other groups, and support their demands no matter how extreme. All groups subordinate their goals and interests to the overriding objective: the destruction of economic power, capitalism and America as we know it. This faction includes various racial and ethnic minorities, radical feminists, gays, lesbians, transsexuals, environmentalists, animal rights activists, anarchists, socialists, communists, anti-globalization activists, anti-American activists, militant Islamists, and many others.

The greedy faction includes all self-serving, advantage-seeking groups. The objectives of all these groups are primarily economic and commercial. Many of these groups are well organized. They often control well defined segments of the economy and they seek to protect their territories and monopolies against any outside encroachment. Some of them are successors of centuries old guilds. Traditional blue collar labor unions are also part of this faction, as are beneficiaries of government programs. The most powerful groups in this faction are the professional classes: lawyers, doctors, professors, teachers, bureaucrats, bankers, and their associates. There are literally hundreds of these groups. This faction is politically less homogeneous and less reliable than the activists. A substantial portion of their members do not understand the political dynamics of the economy and society or their place in it.

There is considerable overlap between the two main factions. Individuals and even groups can have both economic and ideological motivations at the same time. For example, education professionals have a special political function: they control students. For this reason they are the most ideologically committed group within their faction. At the same time their membership in *Minority Bolshevism* also serves their well defined self interests.

Not all members of the various groups in the coalition favor the Left. Ideological and political affiliations are probabilistic, not deterministic. There are gay Republicans and evangelical Democrats. They are, however, distinct minorities within their respective groups.

Both the activist and greedy factions are controlled by radical leaders who are fully committed to New Left values and goals. Thus, group leaders of the greedy faction are just as ideologically motivated as group leaders of the activist faction. The leadership of all groups is fully devoted to the New Left. Consequently, in case of conflict between groups members of the activist faction usually win. This is how and why environmental activists fighting on behalf of a three-inch fish (Delta Smelt) living in the Sacramento River can effectively shut down agriculture in much of California's Central Valley, causing wide-spread unemployment amongst Hispanic farm workers, who are also part of the Minority Bolshevism coalition.

Such conflicts and their resolutions clearly show that Minority Bolshevik leaders often pay only lip-service to the interests of their member groups. Such disputes expose a significant weak point in the theoretical framework of the New Left strategy.

Nevertheless, the New Left coalition is a well constructed strategic alliance. Its various elements control many other groups of society. For example, each profession dominates an entire industry, a substantial sector of the economy. Everybody who is employed in that sector has a vested interest in its protection.

The coalition of all left-wing groups combined has the power to win elections. They don't have a dependable majority yet, but gaining such majority is only a matter of time and persistence. The New Left didn't quite reach the level of political control FDR had. This is partly because the New Left is more openly radical than the New Deal coalition was, and partly because the capitalist economy is in better shape than it was during the Great Depression. To overcome this obstacle the New Left takes advantage of every economic problem and every mistake made by its opponents. Every economic problem is an opportunity for the Left to denounce and damage capitalism. Usually, they don't let crises go to waste. Weakening the US economy is in their interest.

So who are their opponents? Who is not included in the New Left coalition? How are these others different from the left-wing?

The most important opponents of *Minority Bolshevism* are business people, especially small business owners and their families. Lots of non-unionized workers, self-employed people, managers, members of the military and law enforcement officers are more sympathetic to the Right. Followers of traditional religions are ideologically opposed to the New Left. Social conservatives, war veterans, patriots and anti-communists generally prefer right-wing policies. Whites, married people (especially with children), high earners are less likely to support New Left ideologies and policies. People living in the Midwest, in the South and the landlocked middle states are more likely to favor the Right.

The New Left does not have the support of large majorities. Its power base is a carefully assembled alliance of minorities, each under the control of its radical leadership. The interests of every single minority in the New Left coalition directly contradict the interests of the whole, the interests of the country. This is not true of the other side. While the interests and ideology of right-wing groups are not identical, none of them are in direct conflict with those of the country.

Supporters of right-wing policies do now want to harm America. Following their particular interests is not harmful to the whole. Their ideologies do not aim to destroy capitalism. They do not weaken or harm the country.

Serving the interests of the professional classes is objectively damaging the American economy and it may lead to its eventual destruction. This is so even if these professionals don't want to intentionally harm the country.

The New Left coalition is an attempt to achieve political power by uniting disparate minorities whose radical leadership is busy demolishing the very systems, the very countries they seek to rule.

Minority Bolshevism is a hostile coalition assembled from opposing and destructive minorities whose leadership is trying to subvert, sabotage, defeat and overthrow our political and economic systems.

This is the change they can believe in.

Part Eight — Political Principles

8.1 — Freedom and Equality

Both right-wing and left-wing ideology and propaganda proclaim their unquestionable support for traditional American values. The Declaration of Independence and the Preamble of the Constitution list most of these basic principles. They are: equality, unalienable (human) rights, life, liberty, the pursuit of happiness, justice, domestic tranquility, common defence and general welfare.

The Founding Fathers specified only those values that had to be protected and maintained by the government, often from the government itself. They did not list moral principles they considered individual responsibility. Nevertheless, these ancient concepts, these rules of conduct, these basic human beliefs are also very much part of our culture and our national identity. Without them we would be just a bunch of savages. A few of these principles are: honesty, patriotism, compassion, fairness, sensitivity, loyalty, honor, courage, etc.

There are other kinds of values as well.

Different ideologies emphasize different political values. The right-wing generally considers freedom the most important right American citizens have. Leftists typically value equality above all other ideals.

The unalienable rights of life and liberty recognized by the Declaration of Independence are well defined in the Bill of Rights. These rights are secured by constitutional prohibitions imposed on the government. Unfortunately, the meaning of self-evident truth "that all Men are created equal" is not defined by any of the founding documents.

Originally, equality meant equality before the law. The Virginia Declaration of Rights (immediate forerunner to the US Declaration of Independence) says "That all men are by nature equally free and independent..." Unfortunately, the existence and tacit approval of slavery further clouded these issues.

The Left (both old and new) took full advantage of these ambiguities. They used the very important, valid, legitimate, but hopelessly muddled concept of equality as justification for all kinds of social programs and welfare schemes. They regularly invoke equality as a constitutional principle justifying the establishment of Socialism. Clearly, the Founding Fathers have never even contemplated such propositions. Then again, the original intent of the Constitution never really mattered to the Left.

Both the historical context and the internal logic of the founding documents make it crystal clear that economic equality or 'equality of outcomes' was never considered a founding principle of the republic. The very concept of economic equality contradicts and invalidates most of the other founding principles. It does so by obligating society and its members to provide the wealth necessary to make others equally well off.

Admittedly, most people in America and elsewhere show a clear preference for equality, including economic equality, even if they are not certain what that really means or how it might work. The confusion over such a fundamental issue is one of the leading causes of political unrest. The demand for equality is one of the most common reasons for starting wars, riots and rebellions, second only to religion and the 'will of God'.

For better or worse the American people are convinced that all men are created equal, whatever that means. We must make sure that the disputes over the meaning and implementation of equality do not destroy our lives and liberty, and they do not make the pursuit of happiness impossible or meaningless.

No society has ever achieved anything close to real economic equality, although not for the lack of trying. Attempts to impose economic equality always resulted in political oppression. This is a logical outcome of all such efforts. In Khmer Rouge Cambodia all private property, money and markets were abolished. All economic power was destroyed and replaced by political power. Brother Number One (Pol Pot) held the power of life and death. The country turned into killing fields.

This experience was repeated in many other countries where the equality experiment was tried. The French Revolution had the Reign of Terror. Soviet Russia had the Holodomor and the Gulag. Communist China had the Cultural Revolution and reeducation camps. North Korea has no private property, but it did have a *'Great Leader'* followed by his son the *'Dear Leader'*; it did have famine and it does have nuclear weapons. More people were systematically starved to death in the name of equality than any other ideology.

Fighting for equality is a worthwhile goal. This fight, however, must not endanger our other important values, especially freedom. The guarantees of the Bill of Rights should never be violated, not even in the name of equality. Especially, not in the name of equality.

8.2 — Capitalism and Equality

Capitalism and equality seem to be in constant conflict with each other. Capitalism is always on the defensive. Equality seems to be winning, certainly on the ideological battlefields of the culture wars.

The Founding Fathers held the truth to be self evident, "that all men are created equal…" Yet, it is very clear that none of them contemplated the establishment of Socialism, Communism or any kind of economic equality. How can we explain this seemingly obvious contradiction?

The concept of economic equality is a Leftist creation. Its proponents simply misappropriated the concept and the eloquent expression from the Declaration of Independence for their own purposes.

Leftists (both old and new) always ignored the wealth-creating function of Capitalism and emphasized the supposed unfairness of the outcome instead. But fairness is not that simple. No one in his right mind would advocate equal pay for unequal effort. No one in his right mind would pay equal prices for unequal values. No one in his right mind thinks that a Porsche should cost the same as a bicycle. Yet, when it comes to judging the unequal outcomes of capitalist economies many people would make similar nonsensical judgments.

Leftist propaganda uses this inconsistency very effectively. Instead of explaining truthfully how economic values are created, how they are priced and allocated, they question the motives of capitalists. Businessmen are declared greedy. They are assigned one of the deadly sins and they are judged guilty without trial.

Unfortunately, there are many people who do take advantage of others, who exploit others, who acquire wealth without producing anything of value. But judging all entrepreneurs guilty by association is clearly wrong.

Witness the one-sided application of moral judgments, the lopsided and unbalanced questioning of motives. Notice how the words *capitalist* and *businessmen* often preceded by the adjective *greedy,* while left-wing government officials are almost never described as *power-hungry politicians.* Entrepreneurs are rarely called *job creators*, while bureaucrats and politicians are often labeled *public servants.*

Much has been made of the fact that a relatively small minority of people owns a disproportionately large part of economic assets and that they earn a disproportionately large part of national income. This by itself is considered proof of their guilt and their greed. This inequality of ownership and income by itself is considered proof of moral failure of capitalism and — by association — a moral failure of the United States of America and Western Civilization in general.

These arguments and insinuations are based on simplistic Marxist dogma. Capitalism is an economic system. Equality is a social objective and a moral principle. The economic function of capitalism is to create wealth, not to create equality. If capitalism was required to create equality it would cease to exist.

As we have seen the production of wealth necessarily creates economic power. Without economic power there is no wealth creation. Limiting economic power limits wealth creation.

Why is that?

The function of economic power is control, the control over economic forces, the 'means of production' in Marxist lingo. Unequal economic power simply means unequal control over the economy. Only a fool or a dishonest Bolshevik theorist would advocate for the equal distribution of economic power or equal control over the economy. Janitors and managers, workers and owners, receptionists and engineers will never have the same income, the same control, the same wealth, nor should they. If they did, the economy would collapse. It makes no sense for janitors and doctors, secretaries and lawyers, security guards and professors to earn the same or to have the same control over healthcare, the law or education. No sane person would want to receive medical treatment prescribed by a committee of doctors, students, janitors and cafeteria workers. Yet, this is precisely what happened all over China during the Cultural Revolution of Mao Zedong.

Income and wealth inequality is a necessary element of any functioning economy. Economic equality would remove almost all incentives to produce wealth. Economic equality would function as economic entropy.

Any redistribution of income, any "spreading the wealth around", should be done outside the economy. Distorting economic processes, tinkering with economic decisions, introducing political or ideological considerations into capitalism will necessarily lead to inefficiency, to decline in growth rates, to recessions, to poverty and to social upheaval. Then again, this is precisely what the New Bolsheviks aim for.

In reality, Leftists do not really want to equalize incomes, wealth or control. No sociology professor, not even a communist one, seriously wants to be equal (economically or otherwise) with the guy who comes to clean his back yard with a leaf-blower on his back. No diversity coordinator wants her secretary to tell her what to do. No Democratic Party activist wants his driver to control his election strategy.

What do they really want?

They want to take control of the economy. They want political power to replace much of economic power. They want to be able to distribute the wealth produced by others as they see fit. They want to take the money necessary to get elected, rather than beg businessmen for it.

They are not only power hungry, they are also greedy. They are not satisfied with their political and ideological power, they want to control the wealth created by others, too.

How is it more fair for a federal bureaucrat to dictate the terms of a contract between others than for the parties themselves to negotiate those terms? It is not.

How is it fair for government officials to distribute goods produced by others, or as they say "to spread the wealth around"? It is not.

In a free enterprise system you can buy what you need, what you want, what you can afford. If you want more than what you can afford you are free to try and earn more. You are endowed with the unalienable Right of the pursuit of Happiness. If you are unable to earn enough you can ask for help. People and charities inclined to help will do so.

In a socialistic system envisioned by Leftists you will not be able to buy what you want. Your income will be allocated according to the preferences of the holders of political power. Fewer and fewer things will be sold and more and more things will be distributed. It is already happening. It's been happening for quite a long time now.

You cannot just build a house anymore; you need a detailed building permit. Numerous inspections will follow and you will have to pay for them.

You cannot just open a business, you need a license. Most likely several licenses.

You cannot just produce something; you need permission from people who don't produce anything. Children's lemonade stands have been fined and shut down all over the country for violating licensing rules.

You cannot buy a good education. You need to apply for one.

You cannot just go to court to get justice. You need a lawyer. The person who represents himself has a fool for a client. Everyone knows that.

You cannot buy medicine. You need a doctor to prescribe it for you. He will often do that without examining you, as long as you, your insurance company or the taxpayers pay him.

Soon, if you need an operation you will have to apply for one. If you think HMO-s are terrible, wait until they are all run by the government. If you know anyone on Medicaid ask them what it's like.

That is what the slogans of equality will bring you.

8.3 — Freedom and Democracy

Curiously, the confusion regarding equality often appears as a conflict between freedom and democracy. This is all the more strange considering that the word *democracy* does not appear in the Declaration of Independence, in the

Constitution, or in the Bill of Rights. Amazingly, not even the later amendments contain the word *democracy*.

Not mentioning *democracy* in these documents is not so astonishing if we reflect on the fact that the Founding Fathers did not intend to establish a democracy. They wanted to create a republic. None of this prevented President Woodrow Wilson to enter the First World War in order to make "the world safe for democracy". In fact, he was very fond of democracy, both as a political slogan and as a political party. So much so that he signed into law, among other things, the creation of the Federal Reserve Bank and the progressive income tax, both of them enacted by a Democratic Congress.

Just like equality the concept of democracy is often misinterpreted. Democracy actually has several different but valid meanings. Besides these, democracy acquired a new, ideologically loaded meaning in the last century.

Both the concept and the word *democracy* originated in ancient Greece. At that time it simply meant the "rule of the people", as opposed to the rule of kings, the rule of aristocracy or the rule of dictators. In the philosophy of the Enlightenment democracy meant a political system regulating the formation of government. To the Founding Fathers democracy meant the consent of the governed. This principle means that people should be governed by their elected representatives and that the people have the inherent right to change their government.

The principle of democracy has often been used and misused for political and ideological causes. The Democratic-Republican Party was founded by Jefferson and Madison in 1792. Within a half a century Southern slaveholders took control of the party for their own purposes. Increasingly, democracy became used as justification for slavery. According to this view, anything the majority wanted was legitimate, including the preservation and expansion of slavery, even if it meant the dissolution of the Union. Majority vote justified anything and everything. While technically true, this interpretation clearly distorted the principle of democracy into its very opposite.

After the severe economic depression of 1893 the left-wing of the Progressive Movement took control of the Democratic Party. The movement's leader Woodrow Wilson made a diabolical pact with white Southerners. In exchange for their support of his socialistic agenda he tolerated racial segregation. This arrangement endured even under the Franklin Delano Roosevelt administration. The mass migration of African Americans from the segregated South to the industrial North was a direct consequence of the pact made by Wilson. FDR managed to pull the newly unionized Northern blacks into his New Deal coalition, cementing his control over American politics for an entire generation. He was elected and re-elected President for life.

This alliance of disparate groups changed the face of American politics forever. Northern blacks and Southern whites, social progressives and segregationists, Catholics, Jews, labor unions, big city political machines, and eventually even Southern blacks all united under an ideological agenda. This was the first iteration of Minority Bolshevism in the United States of America. It lasted until 1968, when the New Left took control of the Democratic Party. At that time Southern whites left the party, not entirely on their own accord.

The principles of democracy and self-government got more and more distorted under these political arrangements. The principle of democracy unmentioned in the Constitution overshadowed the values expressly articulated by the Founding Fathers. The right to vote became more important than life, liberty and the pursuit of happiness, not to mention justice, domestic tranquility (peace), common defence (security) and general welfare (prosperity). Votes were increasingly exchanged for favors, for support of narrow ethnic, parochial or economic interests.

Both Presidents Wilson and Roosevelt unhesitatingly restricted basic liberties for the sake of political expediency in pursuit of their ideological agendas. They were especially eager to increase taxes, nationalize industries, restrict economic activities, redistribute income and start social programs. Perhaps not coincidentally, each of them also entered a World War, and they both signed international agreements that fundamentally changed global affairs. Wilson was the father of the League of Nations. FDR was the driving force behind the United Nations. Woodrow Wilson was awarded the Nobel Peace Prize.

Much of today's political and economic reality originates with these two men.

Americans consider freedom and democracy their fundamental political values. We go to war to defend freedom and democracy. Most people believe that freedom and democracy are two aspects of the same thing. Unfortunately this belief is mistaken. This misconception is the result of decades long deliberate ideological misrepresentation.

There is considerable conflict between freedom and democracy. In fact, in one aspect they are directly opposed to each other. In another aspect they are mutually supportive constituents of a larger concept articulated by President Lincoln: "...government of the people, by the people, for the people..."

How can freedom and democracy be in conflict with each other?

Democracy is rule of the people. By definition, any rule by anybody is a limitation on freedom. This fact is easy to recognize when a minority rules over the majority. Most of the other words ending in '-cracy' refer to such political arrangements. Aristocracy, theocracy, bureaucracy, plutocracy, technocracy, and other forms of meritocracy designate particular groups who rule their societies. Democracy differs from them in one aspect: it is rule by the majority of the people. To be sure, that is a big difference. Majority rule is almost always preferable to minority rule. But it still is rule and being ruled by someone else is by definition a restriction on freedom.

Furthermore, majority rule can be just as oppressive as minority rule. Slavery in America is a clear example. The oppression of Jews through the centuries is another.

The Constitution of the United States solves this conflict by protecting certain basic rights from government intrusion. Unfortunately, even these constitutional protections have been turned inside out by political correctness, multiculturalism and the introduction of sweeping prohibitions against any kind of discrimination.

There is another significant distortion of the concept of democracy. Most people instinctively recognize and accept the natural limits of basic rights whether these rights and their limits are spelled out or not. They understand that the pursuit of happiness must have its limits. They also acknowledge the impossibility of absolute justice, the irrationality of peace at any price and the impracticability of perfect security.

Americans have debated, studied and regulated the limits of liberty. For more than two centuries governments legislated and courts adjudicated the precise meaning and boundaries of this fundamental constitutional right. Everyone knows that the freedom of speech does not justify yelling fire in a crowded theatre (unless, of course, there is a fire). We all know that more freedom is not always better for the individual or for society.

Even the right to life is not unlimited. Life can be taken away as a punishment for crime. It can be extinguished in war, during riots or by picking a fight with police. It can be terminated by 'partial birth abortion'. The extent of these curtailments on our basic rights is constantly debated.

Democracy is judged by a different standard. We never hear anyone advocating any limits on democracy. No one ever questions the benefits of increasing democracy.

Americans accept as self-evident that more democracy is always better.

There are two aspects of this issue.

Originally, the right to vote was limited. Both a privilege and a right, this precious entitlement was generally restricted to property owning white males twenty-one years of age or older. It was up to the individual states to regulate who could vote. Gradually, voting rights were expanded to include more and more people. This expansion paralleled the increase of the federal government's power versus the states. First the property qualifications were dropped. After the Civil War non-whites acquired the right to vote. Women suffrage followed in 1920. Finally, in 1971 the age limit was dropped to eighteen years.

Most of these expansions were granted by constitutional amendments. Many of them came about as a result of political movements. Blacks got the vote as a result of the Civil War. Women had to fight for their right to vote for several decades. This process is not over. There are significant efforts under way to grant voting rights to non-citizens. Some of them can already vote in certain local elections. Failing that, Latino activists are fighting for amnesty and naturalization of millions of illegal aliens. Liberals would like to guarantee voting rights for convicted felons serving their sentences in prison. Many of these maneuvers are thinly veiled efforts to increase the power base of the Democratic Party.

The other aspect of this issue is voter turnout. It is a well-known fact that a substantial proportion of eligible voters don't vote. In some cases less than half of them actually cast their votes. This seemingly mundane phenomenon obscures a complex, controversial and potentially explosive issue.

The assumption that more democracy is always better suggests that increasing voter turnout is an indisputable good. This conclusion is closely related to the other unquestioned belief that more equality is always better.

Closer examination and rational evaluation reveals that these assumptions are not true. Regrettably, another development further confuses the issue. The massive increase in government control over our lives changed the dynamics of power and democracy.

Democracy mutated from a restriction on government power into its very opposite. It became a tool of using government power to gain advantage. The consent of the governed became the power to redistribute wealth, the power to expropriate someone else's property, the power to grant privileges to certain groups, to "empower them". As a result, more democracy means increased government power and more redistribution. Increasing voter turnout became the means of enforced equalization, the means of taking other people's money (OPM).

In their quest for political power, Minority Bolsheviks promise more government handouts and more democracy to the people, especially to targeted minorities. In reality, however, they are trying to take away from us what we already have: freedom. Every year, *We the people* exchange our precious and shrinking freedoms for vague and unreliable promises.

Prudent observation and simple logic suggests that democracy has an optimum degree, a level where it is the most beneficial. Democracy is not a value in itself; it is a means to an end. As the Declaration of Independence states: "...to secure these rights, Governments are instituted among Men, deriving their just powers from the consent of the governed..." Therefore, the optimum level of democracy is that which institutes the best government attainable under the circumstances. The best government, in turn, is that which secures these rights to the maximum extent possible.

To institute, to elect such a government requires a responsible and well-informed electorate. Not voting is a clear indication that something is wrong. Either the choices presented to potential voters are not palatable (all candidates are bad) or the potential voters themselves don't

159

care enough or don't know enough to bother with voting. Trying to entice ill-informed or uninterested people to vote is clearly counterproductive. This is true regardless how it is done. Using demagoguery, exploiting racial, ethnic or class differences or promising government benefits all have potentially serious negative consequences. Voter registration drives are generally damaging to the very values adopted by the Declaration of Independence and guaranteed by the Constitution and the Bill of Rights. Yet, voter registration drives are commonplace political maneuvers, particularly (but not exclusively) favored by the Left (both old and new). Multilingual ballots proliferate.

Freedom, democracy, equality, welfare, taxation, government regulation, and many other values, principles and standards all have an optimal level. These levels change over time according to objective circumstances (outside forces) and according to the abilities and desires of the people. It is possible to have too much freedom, too much democracy, too much equality; just as it is possible to have too little freedom, not enough democracy and too much inequality.

Democracy is a two edged sword. We have to wield it very carefully and use it only for noble, honest, just and worthy purposes. It is not easy to know what these purposes might be.

8.4 — Democracy — Totalitarianism

The Founding Fathers were right in limiting democracy. What a stable and democratic government really needs is the *consent of the governed* not the fulfillment of all the wishes of the people. Given an opportunity, people will vote for benefits to themselves even if the country cannot possibly afford these. This problem was recognized by the Founding Fathers and many other thinkers who came after them.

When democracy is further distorted to mean the rule of a coalition of minorities additional dangers arise. Such 'identity politics' go far beyond the *consent of the governed*. This coalition of minorities is not the association of free people. It is a pact of the minorities involved, whose members are merely tools serving the purposes of their leaders. The members often cannot comprehend these purposes and they don't understand the nature of the coalition or their own place in it.

Voting for narrow minority interests — while is not good — is not dangerous by itself. What makes it so is the fact that all of these minorities have become subservient to the New Left, an ideologically motivated group, intent to destroy economic power, capitalism and America.

Too much democracy — voting on every conceivable issue, mandating more and more benefits for more and more groups, forbidding more and more behaviors and limiting more and more freedoms — leads to gradually developing totalitarianism. Too much democracy can easily lead to the same place as Soviet Bolshevism and the Dictatorship of the Proletariat did: the place where everything is forbidden, and what is not forbidden is mandatory.

Most people sense this creeping totalitarianism, even if they cannot put their fingers on it. They instinctively know that their freedoms are slowly eroded by an insidious unseen force.

FDR's "freedom from want" is slowly destroying all the freedoms enumerated in our Bill of Rights.

8.5 — The Role of Government

During the last few decades much of the political struggle between *Right* and *Left* revolved around the role of government.

Leftists (both old and new) utilize the government as a versatile tool to acquire, to enlarge and to use political power for their ideological and political purposes. They justify the exponential increase of government power by invoking fairness, social justice, common welfare and democracy.

Many government programs do benefit large numbers of citizens in very real ways. They also make these very citizens dependent on the government programs that benefit them. This dependence, in turn, increases the support for government programs, and magnifies the political power accumulated by the New Left.

Leftists also like to quote the words of President Abraham Lincoln to almost magical effect: "…government of the people, by the people, for the people". Leftists use these words to justify all government programs they favor and to justify the limitless expansion of government power.

Against the Left's massive propaganda effort the Right meekly argues that government is inherently inefficient. They regularly quote Ronald Reagan's famous words: "Government is not the solution to our problem, government is the problem."

While it is true that excessive government power is one of the major problems we face, this is not because it is inefficient. In fact, if we made government more efficient we would have a much bigger problem. This is easy to see in the dual nature of totalitarian governments. Their government agencies and their functions dedicated to secure the power of the rulers are generally extremely efficient. The secret police is always quick and competent. On the other hand, government agencies and functions that supposed to serve the public — and especially the economy — are notoriously slow, inefficient and corrupt. Our own government exhibits the very same dual nature — if not quite as oppressively. Compare the differences in efficiency of the IRS or the US Attorneys versus the inefficiency of the Post Office or countless licensing authorities.

Public bureaucracies, especially inefficient ones, weaken the economy, undermine freedom, and make the population dependent on the government. They also serve the interests of the bureaucrats themselves who acquire more and more power, and the interests of public service unions that benefit at the expense of society in a parasitic fashion. They always serve their own interests quite efficiently.

To paraphrase Ronald Reagan: More efficient government is not the solution to our problem; more efficient government is simply a bigger problem. A much bigger problem. A different problem.

The real issue is the balance of the various kinds of powers. In our age this means the balance between political and economic power. For the Founding Fathers this meant the balance between *church and state*. Their solution was the separation of church and state. Similarly, our solution should be the separation of economic and political power.

Incidentally, control exercised by professional groups and unions over large segments of the economy has the same effect as government regulation: distortion.

As we have seen, political power uses government as a tool. As political power grows at the expense of economic power the holders of this political power increasingly become the ruling elite. As a result of these changes we already have a *government of the elite, by the elite, for the elite.*

Who is this elite?

The New Left and its allies.

How do we know this? Just watch the news. Generals of the armed forces are forced to resign for opposing gays in the military. National security agencies are forbidden to use the expressions of "Islamic terrorist" and "Jihad". Real estate developers are forced to build 'low income housing'. Banks are forced to relax lending standards to selected minorities. Police is forbidden to profile criminal suspects. And on and on and on…

Who is calling the shots?

The New Left and its agents. Their ideology rules.

If this is not enough proof take another look at Leftist theory. Marxists originally considered the government their number one enemy, the faithful servant of capitalism and the bourgeoisie. The revolution of the proletariat was supposed to destroy capitalist governments, replace them with the 'Dictatorship of the Proletariat' and use these dictatorial government powers for its own revolutionary purposes. Once Communism was achieved, however, government — 'the state' — was supposed to "wither away".

Soviet Bolshevism did achieve the first step: it did grab government power and used it very efficiently to destroy its enemies, especially economic power. Stalin and Soviet Bolshevism executed entire social classes that held any economic power. They murdered millions of people because Marxist-Leninist theory required it.

Today's New Bolsheviks, however, no longer consider the government their enemy. On the contrary, the New Left continually tries to increase government power — political power — at the expense of all other powers, especially economic power. This clearly proves that for all practical purposes the New Left has already seized political power. Leftists achieved this (not yet irreversible) victory by lying their way into power, not by armed revolution but by ideology, by "marching through the institutions", by exploiting the weaknesses of democracy. Exactly as Antonio Gramsci had envisioned.

Anti-war protesters of the 1960-s called policemen "pigs". They considered the US Department of Justice one of their main enemies. Now, the DOJ enforces political correctness, multiculturalism and assorted other leftist ideologies. The police became unionized public servants, friends and allies of the New Left in an uneasy and somewhat schizophrenic relationship.

The *Weather Underground* bombed the US Capitol and the Department of State among many other targets. These days the same people who committed these atrocities are friends with politicians, go to cocktail parties with diplomats and endorse electoral campaigns.

These and many other government institutions have been marched through. In fact, they have been trampled over.

8.6 — Taxes, Debts, and Deficits

During the last few decades much of the debate about the role of government revolved around taxes, deficits and debt.

Everyone understands that increasing the role of government costs money. Most people also understand that government does not produce wealth; it merely redistributes wealth created by others. In a free enterprise system these *others* are known as the private sector.

None of this means that government is useless. On the contrary, a well-managed government is essential for a healthy society and a healthy economy.

Leftists assert that one of the most important functions of government is to provide welfare for the inhabitants of the country, citizens and non-citizens alike. They often quote the Preamble of the US Constitution to prove their point, even though the relevant passage actually states that one of the purposes to establish the Constitution was "to *promote* the general Welfare", not to provide such welfare. Indeed, for a long time the federal government did not provide welfare, general or otherwise to anyone. Nevertheless, this distinction is lost on most people.

Progressives, liberals, New Deal socialists and assorted other Leftists never ceased their efforts to turn America into a welfare state. Today most federal spending is to pay for various entitlement programs benefiting various groups.

These expenditures, of course, have to be financed somehow. The two main sources of federal *revenues* are taxes and borrowings. Democrats and Republicans have been fighting over taxes, deficits and debts seemingly forever.

These fights distract our attention from what really matters, the control over the economy.

The economy produces wealth. The government spends an ever increasing amount of money for various purposes. Much of this government spending is a simple redistribution of the national income. Most of this redistribution is required by law, entitling the beneficiaries to receive regular payments from the government (entitlement programs). Once such entitlement programs are in place, it is politically impossible to stop them. *We the people* are stuck with the promises the government made. There are political fights between Right and Left over new entitlement proposals. Existing entitlements, however, are never seriously threatened. Most politicians pay lip service to entitlement reform. Yet, at the end of each year we always have more entitlement programs in place than we had before.

Whether we pay for government spending from taxes or we borrow money to do so is largely irrelevant in the long run. Whether we spend our national income or merely mortgage our future earnings will not change the final outcome. We are losing ground in either case. The ground we losing is the economy.

New Left theorists know this full well. The welfare state was designed to a large extent to destroy capitalism. As the saying goes: "the power to tax is the power to destroy". To this we can add: the power to borrow is the power to destroy.

Perversely, we are watching our future unfolding in front of our very eyes, without really understanding what's going on. The welfare states of Europe are struggling for survival. We are just a few years behind them. Greece, Spain, Italy and the others are us.

We have spent all our savings. What we didn't spend we lost on financial speculation. We have literally bought much of our prosperity on credit. We owe the Chinese for the iPhones they manufactured and we owe Saudi Arabia for the oil produced there. We even borrowed the profits they made selling us their products. We borrowed from the past and we borrowed from the future. We owe mortgages on the houses we live in, often more than their value.

We have borrowed and spent all Social Security and Medicare taxes collected by the government. **We have pawned our own future entitlements**. Think about that for a minute.

Money is normally generated by economic activity, by producing wealth. Banks, (including the Federal Reserve) facilitate the circulation of money. This circulation includes commercial transactions (payments), savings, lending, investments and financing. All the money in circulation — whatever its source — represents a demand against the wealth produced. Banks (including the Federal Reserve) do not produce wealth. The money issued by the Federal Reserve is borrowed. It must be paid back. Most of this money is borrowed by Commercial and Investments banks. They need it to replace savings that were spent or to replace investments and bad loans that were lost. The Federal Reserve is lending this money to the banks very cheaply in order to increase demand in the economy. **We are borrowing demand from the future**. Whatever product we buy today with this borrowed money we will not be able to buy tomorrow. We are reducing future demand. We are creating a future recession.

Not only that, but much of this artificially created demand is for foreign products. By borrowing more and more we are helping the Chinese economy more than we are helping our own.

The "dual mandate" of the Federal Reserve (to achieve maximum employment and price stability) is a recipe for disaster. It calls for contradictory actions. It also opens the door for political manipulation of monetary policy and the economy. Political manipulation of the economy — by definition — increases political power to the detriment of economic power.

New Left theorists love this vicious circle. It weakens the economy, it damages the free enterprise system and it increases political power. Most political power accumulates for the benefit of the Left, at least for now.

Taxes, deficits and debts are all consequences of government spending. Whether we pay for this spending now with our taxes or we pay for it in the future the consequences are the same. Political power increases at the expense of economic power. Minority Bolshevism benefits either way.

8.7 — Jews — Anti-Semitism

Historically, major social upheavals always generate an upsurge in anti-Semitism.

Over the millennia Jews have been accused of countless acts of wrongdoing and misbehavior. They have also been accused of doing the exact opposite of those acts. They have been punished and persecuted for both.

Jews have been denounced as ruthless capitalists and as dogmatic communists. They were blamed for being bloodsucking bankers and for being socialist revolutionaries. They were criticized as rootless cosmopolitans and as Zionist nationalists.

The Romans oppressed them because they had only one God. Later on, Roman armies persecuted the Jews as Christians and crucified Jesus as King of the Jews (I.N.R.I.). On the other hand, the Christians themselves blamed the Jews for killing Jesus. Muslims think that Jews betrayed their own God. Nazi Germany tried to exterminate them. The Palestinians want to send them back to Russia and Germany.

Are any of these accusations true?

Yes and no. There are and there were Jewish capitalists and communists, bankers and revolutionaries, patriots and internationalists. Jews may follow orthodox, conservative or reform Judaism. They can be Christians or Buddhists. Many of them are atheists. They are patriotic Frenchmen, Englishmen and Americans.

No matter what they do, however, someone will hate them for it, especially if they do it well, which is often the case.

In the last few years (as before) much has been made of the fact that most American Jews tend to support liberal causes and left-wing politicians. Undeniably, Jews overwhelmingly vote for Democratic Party candidates. They donate lots of money to leftist organizations.

Exasperated right-wing Jews have been trying to figure out the reasons for this behavior. They pointed out that Jews were historically just as conservative as any other group, if not more so. They also tried to psychoanalyze Jewish liberalism. They offered various explanations, none of them particularly enlightening or attractive.

This book is mainly concerned with the rise of the New Left. It scrutinizes all aspects of left-wing policies, participation, organization, power structure, goals and methods. Thus, it is necessary to clearly state the role of American Jews in contemporary politics, to shed light on their causes and motivations for supporting the New Left.

Normally, such commentary should be reserved for representatives of the group involved. The only reason this chapter was written is the lack of credible explanation and the desperate need for it. The difficulty seems to lie in the deliberately camouflaged structure of Minority Bolshevism.

Throughout history Jews often faced impossible choices, problems that had no good solutions. They frequently found themselves in situations where their social position predetermined their actions. They simply tried to satisfy the requirements confronting them. When they were told to assimilate they tried to assimilate, when they were segregated they lived in the ghetto, when they were forbidden from owning land they opened shops, etc. Shylock was a banker because Christians — who were not allowed to lend money at interest — needed a Jew to do the job for them.

In contemporary America (and elsewhere) Jews are attracted to the professions. They value education. They also live in big cities near the coasts. Jewish culture, religion and tradition prescribe and sanction community action, mutual help and charity. Traditionally, many Jews are employed in entertainment related fields, music, theatre, comedy, movies and so on.

Following Antonio Gramsci's prescription the New Left targeted these very fields. Achieving *cultural hegemony* required an attack on education and culture. The *culture war* of the New Left invaded the very areas where Jews were congregating. The New Left coalition co-opted the professional classes to build up its *Minority Bolshevism*. Jews lived in big coastal cities; they studied at universities and became professionals. They lived on the battlefields of the *culture war* and their turf was invaded by the New Left. It is not surprising that they became overwhelmingly liberal. A large percentage of them were members of the targeted groups. Systematic brainwashing finished the job. Gentiles who were in the same positions were affected the same exact way. The same (very high) proportion of university educated big city professionals living near the coasts is liberals and leftists, regardless whether they are Jews or Gentiles.

We should not make the mistake of judging people according to their ethnic or religious backgrounds. Such an error would directly benefit the New Left who are masters of identity politics. The culprit is the philosophy, the ideology, not the people infected with it. Blacks, Latinos, Jews, feminists, lawyers, doctors, gays and others are both victims and soldiers in this struggle. We need to make them understand the nature of *Zombie Communism*, to make them see how *Minority Bolshevism* operates.

Our enemies are the hard core ideologists, the conspiring theorists who know and understand what they are doing, who deliberately want to destroy capitalism and America as we know it. We need to defeat these people whoever they are, regardless of their ethnicity or their religion. Their backgrounds should serve neither as justification nor as excuse for their guilt.

Marxists, Bolsheviks, communists are our enemies whoever they are. That is the only criterion they should be judged by.

Part Nine — Suicide of Soviet Bolshevism

9.1 — Zombie Communism

There is another important aspect of the current political and ideological struggle. It is a well hidden connection that we need to recognize if we want to understand the problems Western Civilization is facing.

The conflict between left- and right-wing politics and ideology is well known. Countless books and articles have been written about this subject. Politicians, journalists, analysts and ordinary citizens carefully watch every movement of their opponents. Everything is documented, discussed and analyzed. We all know what is happening in front of our eyes. We think we understand what is going on behind the scenes.

It is also generally accepted that one of the biggest conflicts of the 20th Century was the competition between Communism and capitalism. This contest was represented by the superpower rivalry between the Soviet Union and the United States of America. At the height of the conflict global thermonuclear war and complete annihilation of all civilization seemed entirely possible. Yet, just a few years later the communists threw in the towel. The Soviet Union suddenly and unexpectedly collapsed. Capitalism and free markets have seemingly triumphed. Socialism and collectivism were discredited, seemingly forever.

America celebrated. We cashed our "peace dividend" check and we promptly spent all the money and more. We cut back on military spending. We took a vacation from history. History was offended. It didn't like to be ignored. A dozen years after the demise of our deadliest enemy we were attacked by Islamic terrorists on September 11, 2001. By the end of the decade our economy lay in ruins. The real estate market collapsed. The world-wide banking system stopped working. Suddenly, we were at the edge of the abyss, looking at a total economic catastrophe. The arrival of the second Great Depression was announced. (See Exhibit Two.)

Ferocious left-wing activists appeared out of nowhere. They denounced capitalism as an utter failure. They attacked free markets as unfair and inefficient. They accused America of exploiting the working classes, victimizing Third World countries and destroying the environment. They condemned the financial markets, multi-national corporations, American imperialism, globalization, consumerism and the profit motive.

They demanded change. Socialism returned from the dead, this time in America, of all places. This Zombie Communism (New Left) seems almost indestructible.

How could this happen?

To understand this apparent anomaly we have to go back four generations or so.

9.2 — Prophecy

Under one interpretation (#1), Zombie Communism is a direct descendent of Marxism-Leninism, while Stalinism was only a bastard grandchild of Marxism, a mistake, a historical detour.

Under a different interpretation (#2), not only Stalinism, but Leninism also was a bastard child of Marxism, and Zombie Communism is the only legitimate descendent of the real — idealized — Marxism, the collectivist, socialist philosophy, the much prophesized savior of the working classes.

Thus, we face a familiar conundrum: who is the real Messiah?

As we have seen earlier (in chapter 5.1), Karl Marx predicted that Communism would triumph in the economically most developed countries. He believed that it was necessary for capitalism to fully develop, to become world-wide imperialism **before** Communism could finally

173

defeat it. He taught that the economic base (*the mode of production*) fundamentally determined the *superstructure* (legal, political relations and class consciousness). Unfortunately, the German Kaiser Wilhelm II threw a monkey wrench into the machinery of prophesized history.

Under interpretation #2, the Kaiser not only derailed the future envisioned by Karl Marx but also condemned the Communist movement itself to take a century long detour. As a side-effect he almost annihilated Germany itself.

9.3 — Monster Births

The prematurely born Soviet Union grew up to be a monster. Its fatal birth defects almost destroyed the world. More importantly (for true believers) it crippled the very movement that was supposed to end history (*prehistory*). Brutal Bolshevik bullies didn't only kill the Czar and his family, didn't only eliminate kulaks, capitalists and financiers; they executed many communist intellectuals and theorists. Lenin's Bolsheviks were massacring their fellow revolutionaries in Kronstadt just as celebrations of the 50th anniversary of the Paris Commune got under way.

KGB (OGPU, NKVD, etc.) thugs and Comintern agents systematically murdered all independent minded communists (both Eastern and Western) to ensure the victory and supremacy of Stalinism. In the Soviet Union even Stalinist cadres were periodically purged as a matter of totalitarian efficiency. According to this interpretation, Stalin almost completely eradicated Marxism.

The rise of Hitler and the Second World War stopped this process, at least temporarily. One madness neutralized another madness. Stalin dissolved the Comintern at the insistence of Churchill and FDR. He had to concentrate on his own survival and he needed help from his Western allies. This was one of several paradoxical events that made the scenic route to proletarian utopia so exciting.

174

Soon after WWII ended the Cold War broke out. Socialists and communists in the West were fighting a losing battle against capitalism, but at least they were reasonably safe from Stalin and his newly invigorated KGB agents. This was another one of those paradoxes.

9.4 — Resurrection

Western Marxism slowly recovered. Stalin died in 1953, but most organized socialist and communist parties of the West remained under Soviet control. But out of sight a new movement was stirring. Actually, it wasn't really a new movement. It was a revival of original Marxism. It rose from the ashes of the German communist movement crushed by the onslaught of Nazism and Stalinism. Its leading theorists, affiliated with the Frankfurt Institute for Social Research (known as the Frankfurt School), recognized the dangers of emerging Nazism just in time. They were also smart enough not to seek asylum in Soviet Russia. They found refuge in FDR's America and Columbia University. During WWII some of them worked for US intelligence agencies (OSS); others were involved in such activities only informally.

After the war they resumed their original careers as professional Marxists, this time in the USA. They were the founding fathers of the New Left. The first generation of American New Left leaders studied at the feet of these German communists. Many of their works were published in America and translated into numerous languages. After things settled down they expanded their activities into postwar Europe, especially England and Germany.

9.5 — Growing Pains

The New Left had a tense relationship with Soviet dominated communist parties and other organizations. Many of the most enthusiastic young revolutionaries were attracted to New Left ideas and philosophies. The New Left, however, didn't have the organizational skills, the material resources and infrastructure to strike out on its own. As a result, an uneasy cooperation developed between the KGB and radical leftist movements.

The German Red Army Faction, the Italian Red Brigades and many other, lesser known organizations started up as New Left movements. After carrying out a few terrorist attacks they desperately needed help. Help mysteriously materialized. They were offered money, weapons, intelligence, safe houses, fake passports and tactical support. Soviet controlled Third World revolutionary movements provided training for them in their guerrilla bases. In turn, they did dirty jobs for the KGB and others. They also provided very useful intelligence to the Soviets.

New Left centers of ideology were also infiltrated by KGB types. Left-wing student organizations, racial or gender based movements, anti-war groups, hippies and others were all vulnerable to Soviet manipulation. International environmental conferences, youth festivals, Third World liberation movements were all controlled from Moscow.

All of this is well known. The other side of the coin, however, is largely unknown and poorly understood.

9.6 — Growing Old

The Soviet Union always had major problems. This was not surprising given the economic and social backwardness of Russia and the ravages of the Bolshevik Revolution and the Second World War. Stalin exterminated most of Russia's intelligentsia, the most productive sector of its peasantry, all of its industrialists, the general staff of its military and everybody else who dared to complain or just looked suspicious. What was surprising, however, that even after Stalin's death the situation didn't improve all that much. In some ways, it actually deteriorated.

The Soviet Union became a military superpower and an international super villain, but its economy was in shambles. This was a forbidden subject, however, as economic and social statistics were considered state secrets. Official propaganda painted a rosy picture that nobody really believed, but very few dared to question. Yet, these facts were very troubling to a small but influential group within the Soviet Communist Party leadership. The **theorists** had a problem. What they knew was incompatible with what they believed, with what they desperately wanted to believe. The theory didn't agree with reality. Too bad for reality, many of them thought.

First, they tried to explain away the problem. They blamed the failures on Stalin, on bad weather, on American imperialism, on sabotage. But even after taking everything into consideration the problems persisted. Leninist dogma was unquestionable and untouchable. Despite all their efforts to damage capitalism and America they were falling further and further behind. It took an increasing share of their national income just to keep up with the United States military. If the trend continued the Soviet economy was destined to fail.

9.7 — The Guardians

Only two groups of people had unlimited access to foreign publications in the Soviet Union. KGB agents needed to know what was happening in order to do their job. They had to read everything so they could effectively infiltrate and fight their enemies, foreign and domestic. They were the guardians of the party and the state.

The other privileged group, the theorists, was in charge of ideology. They had to know what everybody was saying in order to effectively argue with it or effectively lie about it. They also had to make sure that everyone followed the path laid out by Marx, Engels and Lenin. They were the guardians of the prophecy.

What these people were reading was alarming. It was clear to any rational observer that Soviet Communism was inferior to capitalism in many ways. Economic competition with the West was destined for failure. The KGB leadership took comfort in their own superior abilities. They firmly believed that sooner or later they could beat the West by bigger and better clandestine operations. The military wasn't so sure.

The theorists were far more troubled. What disturbed them the most was the criticism coming from New Left theorists of the West. Very smart, committed communists were saying that the Soviet experiment was a mistake from the very beginning. They were showing that all the aberrations of Soviet history, including Lenin's Red Terror and Stalin's purges, were natural consequences of theoretical and ideological errors. Nothing worries a theorist more than the discovery of theoretical errors.

9.8 — Reform Attempts

The Soviet leadership attempted to make a course correction. They liberalized their economy to a certain extent. They allowed their East Block satellite countries to experiment economically and socially. They eased back on military and political confrontation with the West. Détente was born. Cultural exchanges proliferated. Western consumer goods were allowed into some communist countries. Artists and writers enjoyed a little more freedom. Arms control summits were held and treaties were signed.

Leninist hardliners were not amused. The facts seemed to be on their side. Despite all liberalization efforts the Soviet economy fell further behind. The new freedoms made people both more resentful and more willing to criticize the system. The pressure from the West didn't decrease. Some western groups were saying nice things about the Soviet Union but they always had such "useful idiots". The Soviet military was suspicious of all the agreements and treaties.

The West started to make new demands. They were pressing human rights issues, they wanted Soviet Jews to be able to emigrate and dissidents released from prison. The

Americans were using trade as a weapon to achieve their aims. Soviet hardliners knew this could not go on. They had to strike back.

9.9 — Counter-Reformation

On Christmas Eve, 1979 the Soviet Union invaded Afghanistan. Détente was dead. More international trouble soon followed.

Ronald Reagan was elected President. He was no left-winger, but he had something common with the New Left. Both believed that Soviet Communism was a historical error. Reagan decided to correct it. He increased the pressure tremendously, both militarily and economically.

Soviet theorists were frightened. They became more convinced than ever that the Soviet Union was on the wrong track. There was precious little they could do. Rigid old party secretaries, KGB thugs and Red Army commissars held all the cards. They jealously guarded their power. At least the theorists were not exterminated or purged from the party like they would have been under Stalin, a generation before. But they needed help.

9.10 — Blast from the West

Help arrived from an unlikely source.

Rival theorists of the American New Left had their own problem. They were remarkably successful promoting their version of Marxism. They managed to assemble a powerful new coalition. They were on the offensive on all fronts in virtually all Western countries. They achieved *cultural hegemony* prescribed by Gramsci. They were financially secure, socially dominant, politically successful and ideologically self-confident. But they faced a dilemma. Remarkably, their problem was the same as that of their counterparts, the Soviet theorists, namely the Soviet Union itself.

No matter how successful the New Left was they could never overcome one fundamental obstacle. No matter how many young activists they managed to rally for their cause the Right had one ultimate weapon. No matter what arguments the New Left made the Right could always point to the Soviet Union and ask a simple question: Is this what you want? Do you want America to be like the Soviet Union? Do you want your children to live like that?

The New Left didn't have a good answer. Nobody wanted to live like that. Nobody wanted America to be like the Soviet Union (except a few crazies). The New Left tried to explain away the differences, but the arguments were much too convoluted and much too easy to defeat. If Marxism was to ever triumph the Soviet Union had to disappear. That was easier said than done.

Luckily, the New Left had a very powerful weapon. They had good connections. Their *cultural hegemony* enabled them to mingle with high society, including politicians. In fact, many politicians were supporting the New Left, some consciously, some unknowingly; some openly, some covertly. A few of these politicians had good connections in the Soviet Union. There were many other sympathizers, artists, writers, professors, journalists and even some business people.

9.11 — Back Channels

Since the Roosevelt Administration, at least a few channels of communications were always open to the Soviet Union. These "back channels" were very useful for making deals away from public scrutiny. They facilitated spy swaps. They enabled economic cooperation and trade. They were necessary to periodically defuse bitter political conflicts or military standoffs. The New Left used these channels in an attempt to repair Marxism.

They used the same methods that were proven effective in their struggle for *cultural hegemony* in America. They engaged their Soviet theorist counterparts on the cultural and education fields. In communist countries all publications were censored. Copy machines were banned. To reproduce even a single page required approval and registration. Yet, in this environment banned books were regularly printed by the Communist Party itself. Individually numbered copies were distributed to party cadres and trusted intellectuals. New Left publications printed in the West were much in demand behind the Iron Curtain. Secret government agencies translated, published and distributed these works in Eastern Bloc countries.

Travel was trickier. Even high ranking communist officials often defected to the West given a chance. This was highly embarrassing for communist countries. To prevent defections travel to the West was severely restricted. Relatives were held as hostages to ensure the return of travelers. Visiting East Bloc countries was also difficult and often unpleasant.

With a concerted effort the New Left and their Soviet Bloc counterparts managed to overcome these obstacles. They made reasonable compromises with each other and with communist authorities. They established a continuous dialogue and a permanent forum to exchange ideas and strategies. They enlisted sympathetic politicians from both sides. They even recruited rich financiers and other businessmen.

9.12 — Persuasion

Left-leaning American politicians and institutions provided material and logistical support and political cover. The Fulbright Program financed and facilitated student and scholar exchanges. It provided fellowships to selected individuals. East German border guards were still shooting defectors on the Berlin Wall, but at the same time East Bloc Marxist intellectuals were studying at American and Western European universities, financed by capitalist money.

Communist authorities looked the other way. For the most part, after all, it was their own children who traveled to the West on such scholarships. Attitudes slowly changed. Ideas spread. As the superpower arms race was heating up and the war was raging in Afghanistan a new understanding was developing behind the scenes. Old and New Left were converging and they were about to reach a consensus.

New initiatives were introduced to accommodate the growing need for face to face communications. To circumvent still cumbersome travel restrictions, to evade suspicious bureaucrats and to save money alternate locations were utilized. The Soros Foundation established a foothold in Eastern Europe. It was much easier for citizens of Eastern Bloc countries and the Soviet Union to travel there. Conferences and seminars were held.

The Reagan Doctrine was putting a lot of pressure on the Soviet Union from the outside. The Afghan war was also straining its resources to the breaking point. Eastern Europeans were grumbling. The Old Guard was literally dying out. All the while the children of communist intelligentsia were learning the basics of democracy and free markets. They were getting ready. They were quietly hoping for change.

Slowly but surely Soviet theorists came around. One by one they were persuaded and finally convinced that Leninism was just as misguided as Stalinism. They could clearly see that there was no light at the end of their tunnel. The Soviet Union and Leninism had to die so that Marxism of the New Left could live and prosper. For most of them this was a terrible realization. A century of dreams, sacrifices and rivers of blood were all just a mistake, a theoretical error. Now they had to make a wrenching decision.

9.13 — Pulling the Plug

The final verdict had to come from the very top. Ever since the death of Stalin the Soviet Union was governed by collective decisions. To reach such an agreement, first the top theorist, the chief ideologist himself had to be convinced. Most likely he was one of the few old timers who lived through the beginning decades of the Bolshevik Revolution and survived Stalin's purges. He, in turn, had to convince and get approval from the KGB bosses and to secure the agreement of the majority of Central Committee Secretaries. This process took years of carefully shuffling Communist Party leadership. The theorists probably came around by the early 1980's. A few Politburo leaders were on board a year or so later. The rest of the collective leadership took a while longer. The few who resisted were edged out of power or sidelined. It is highly unlikely that either the chief theorist-ideologist or the head of the Communist Party lived to see the changes they approved. They couldn't bear it. By the time Gorbachev became General Secretary of the Communist Party they were both dead.

After the Chernobyl nuclear disaster the changes accelerated. It became increasingly clear to everyone in leadership positions that the Soviet Union was dying. The collective leadership did what it had to do. These inevitable decisions were supported by the majority, but they were not unanimous. Only a handful of the leaders involved understood the meaning and the ramifications of their actions. It is doubtful that Gorbachev himself entirely comprehended what was happening.

9.14 — Suicide

The collapse of the Soviet Union was spectacular. It was the second time in half a century that an empire gave up without a fight. (The other one, the British Empire had help too, also from America.) The awesome military power that for forty years threatened the survival of humanity quickly disintegrated. The mighty Communist Party of the Soviet Union ceased to exist. The Soviet Union dissolved itself.

The New Left managed to pull off a trick never before seen in history. They argued a superpower into committing suicide. That just shows you how dangerous they really are.

The dismantling of the Communist Empire took years. Armies had to be moved and demobilized, governments rebuilt, economies restructured, societies reorganized. Meanwhile, peace had to be maintained and guaranteed. The United States had to be pacified. The New Left didn't really want capitalism and America to triumph. In fact, the New Left wanted them to fail, spectacularly, if possible. This project, however, had to wait for another dozen years to gather steam.

9.15 — Deals

New Left theorists and their Soviet counterparts made a grand bargain. This was necessary to secure the support of the Soviet leadership, to avoid a military takeover and to keep ordinary people calm so they could get used to their new lives.

The grand bargain provided personal security and immunity from prosecution for members of the Communist Party. The deal also enabled members of the ruling groups to retain most of their power but in a different form. Most (but not all) of their political power was converted into economic power. State-run enterprises were sold to politically well-connected individuals, often to the very same communist leaders who ruled the country just before the collapse. In many cases the old leaders retired on guaranteed and comfortable pensions while their children and other family members 'privatized' government property. They financed their purchases with cheap credit provided by the government itself. These newly minted entrepreneurs in turn supported the changes and the emerging political system.

Special attention had to be paid to the military. It was huge and powerful, if unwieldy. On the other hand, generals and officers were always under the strict control of the

Communist Party. Still, it was much safer to separate the soldiers from their guns and other equipment. This had to be done in a hurry. The resulting rapid demobilization was spectacular. Soldiers and officers returning to Russia from Eastern Europe sold their weapons, their uniforms, even their medals on the black markets for a fraction of their cost. Military bases and equipment were abandoned. Navy ships were scuttled. Special Forces barely secured nuclear weapons. Russia was entirely defenseless and vulnerable.

Amazingly, the US was behaving in a compassionate, considerate and benign manner.

The KGB leadership fully supported the changes. Many of the rank and file, however, were dismayed. They were very much against the incomprehensible assault on the essence of Soviet power, but they were helpless to do anything about it. The centralized hierarchy turned against the organization itself blinding all its members. It took an entire generation to partially repair the damage done to the KGB.

Clueless members of the Old Guard resisted. They decided to try one more time to save the Soviet Union. They attempted a *coup d'état* against their nemesis Gorbachev in August 1991. They walked into a carefully designed trap. This pathetic conspiracy provided a perfect excuse to crack down on all elements opposing the changes.

9.16 — The Hidden Conflict

The Cold War seemed like the great conflict between East and West, between capitalism and Communism, between the Soviet Union and the United States of America. But in reality, this was only one aspect of a historical struggle. The other aspect was the conflict within the Left, between Marxism and Leninism-Stalinism, between Soviet Bolshevism and New Left Bolshevism. Capitalism and American Imperialism only won the Cold War by unwittingly serving the interests of an even deadlier enemy, a much more potent version of the same plague, Neo-Marxist Communism.

9.17 — Triumph of the New Left Conspiracy

With the collapse of the Soviet Union the center of Marxism, the center of Leftism shifted back to the West, where it was born and where Karl Marx prophesized it would triumph.

Capitalism rested on its laurels. America took a vacation from history. The New Left went to work immediately. During the decade after the fall of the Soviet Empire the cancer of Communism metastasized and spread all over Western societies, eating away at their economies, their communities, their institutions and their culture. All the while we were celebrating our 'victory' and drank to the "end of history".

The process described in this section is what makes our Exhibit 2 unique. Unlike the other two historic events (and many others) the collapse of the Soviet Union was not an unforeseeable accident. On the contrary, it was a carefully planned and executed operation whose planners misled virtually everyone involved or affected.

Admittedly, the above scenario is an unproven hypothesis. It will surely be denounced as a crazy conspiracy theory. Luckily, however, there is plenty of evidence available to prove or disprove these allegations. There are numerous witnesses, minutes of meetings, orders issued to military and security forces, etc. These events had plenty of victims who saw but did not understand what was happening. Their revelations and memoirs will be crucial in uncovering the truth. Only the dots need to be connected.

9.18 — Historical Analogies

Interestingly, there is a historical analogy to these events. For several centuries Christianity (both Roman Catholicism and Byzantine Orthodoxy) struggled with its most dangerous outside enemy, Islam. Indeed, the rise of

Islam was a major factor of the final disintegration of the Roman Empire, both Western and Eastern. As Muslim navies blockaded the Mediterranean trade with the Orient collapsed, fatally wounding the European empires of Antiquity. The remnants of Western Civilizations fought against Muslim armies of Moors in Spain and against invading Ottoman armies in the East.

It was a life and death struggle.

Yet, there was another struggle within Western Christianity itself, possibly more important in the long run. This was an ideological conflict, known as the Reformation. There are many similarities between the Reformation and the New Left, and their respective battles with their ideological predecessors. There are also significant differences between them, most importantly the fact that actual wars were fought by the forces of Reformation and Catholicism. Also, Catholicism was not destroyed by the Reformation, only pushed back to the east and the south. That fight ended in a draw.

Still, the success of Reformation was essential for the rise of Western Europe, just as the demise of Soviet Communism was necessary for the ascent of the New Left, the triumph of Western Bolshevism.

Another notable historical event was the almost complete abandonment of Maoist Communism by the Chinese Communist Party at the same time when Soviet Bolshevism collapsed. We know who engineered the Chinese reforms: the "Eight Elders" led by Deng Xiaoping whose life had interesting parallels to that of Antonio Gramsci. The Chinese reforms also involved a major restoration of economic power, which was liberated from the complete dominance and control of political power. But that is another story.

None of the comparisons between the Reformation and the New Left, China and the Soviet Union imply any moral judgment or moral equivalence. The point is to examine and understand these events and the forces behind them, not to justify the motives of their proponents or validate the consequences of their actions.

Part Ten — Conclusions

10.1 — What's Wrong with Socialism?

All these accusations against Communists, Bolsheviks, Socialists and other Leftists beg the question: *What is wrong with Socialism?*

Isn't equality a laudable goal, a long-established principle of basic human rights?

Shouldn't society take care of the poor, the sick and the less fortunate?

Shouldn't our economy benefit all members of society?

Isn't it wrong for the rich to exploit the poor?

If so, then what is wrong with socialism?

Inequality, poverty, sickness and exploitation are real problems that have plagued humanity for millennia. There are many other such seemingly intractable problems. We should not deny their existence, nor should we belittle their importance. We shouldn't neglect them and we should not cease our efforts to solve them.

Socialism, however, gives a false solution for such problems.

Socialists believe that almost all social problems are caused by private property. They believe that by abolishing private property and thereby destroying economic power they can cure most ills of society. This way of thinking is much older than Marxism and this opinion was held by many disparate groups throughout history. The *have-nots* always resented the *haves*. They still do and they always will.

Socialists are generally smart enough to recognize that if private property was abolished something would have to take its place. Most of them realize that the economy would not function in anarchy. Society itself would self-destruct.

(Yet, there are still anarchists out there, who advocate just that.)

Most socialists believe that some form of common or community property would be the ideal solution to all these problems. Many more other people also believe this. Most of them are especially concerned with the ownership of productive assets, assets that can produce profits. They advocate social ownership of these assets, known by (Marxist) social science as the "means of production". (Soviet Bolshevism went much farther than that. It abolished all private property, including private ownership of housing and other personal effects. In Cambodia, the Khmer Rouge even abolished money.)

Many varieties of such *social ownership* had been tried over the centuries. Religious communities, co-operatives, kibbutzim, communes and others all tried to create viable enterprises without private property. Marxists, Bolsheviks and Communists all settled on centrally-planned, government-owned production as the ultimate solution.

None of these schemes worked. As Margaret Thatcher famously said: "The problem with socialism is that you eventually run out of other people's money."

The only form of commonly owned productive enterprise that worked in the long run was the joint stock company. (We have discussed that above, under the title *Publicly Held Corporations* in Chapter 4.6.) These corporations work precisely because they did not do away with private property; they only combined privately owned property into a much larger enterprise managed by professional intermediaries. Even these corporations, however, have problems associated with their common ownership structure.

Socialism does not work because *social ownership* does not work.

But why not?

The theory of socialism is based on an inaccurate diagnosis. Society's ills are not caused by private property (or any other institution); they are caused by the faults in human nature. Unjust social institutions and structures are not the causes of injustice, faulty human nature is. The widely perceived injustice of private property itself is an effect of faulty human nature and not the cause of the injustice. The idea that we can cure faulty human nature and the ills of society by manipulating economic structures is a delusion, and a very persistent one. It is also very destructive.

Interestingly, in another context something similar had actually been achieved. Most civilizations going back to antiquity had done away with society-wide polygamy. The institution of monogamy largely cured the immense problem of widespread inability of finding a mate and procreating. Societies that still practice polygamy usually view women as private property or the means of acquiring other valuable assets. On the other hand, families based on monogamous marriage served as the basic building blocks of most civilized societies for thousands of years. Monogamous marriage and the family are far from perfect, but they are essential to any functioning society. No workable replacement of monogamous marriage has been invented yet.

Incredibly, New Left ideology (based on Marxist dogma) is doing everything it can to destroy this most important building block of social equality and economic survival. Even more astonishing is the New Left's tacit approval of polygamy practiced in Muslim societies in the name of multiculturalism. They are also largely silent on the mistreatment of women in Islam. The New Left's real motivation, of course, is purely tactical and self-serving: they need Islam as an ally against their biggest enemy, the 'Great Satan', the United States of America.

Marxist and leftist dislike of monogamy and the family is another theoretical error. Marx and Engels thought that the family was primarily an economic phenomenon and as such it will "wither away" when Communism arrives, along with private property and the 'state'. Bolsheviks could not resist the temptation to speed up history and tried to hasten the demise of the family.

Monogamy and the family, however, are primarily not economic institutions even though they do have major economic effects. Principally, they govern personal relationships, not economic ones. They are social institutions.

Unfortunately, there is no economic equivalent of monogamy. There is no workable institution to solve the problem of economic inequality. All large scale efforts throughout history to limit private property led at best to economic stagnation and at worst to economic and social catastrophes. Indeed, it seems certain that economic inequality is absolutely necessary for the creation of wealth beyond subsistence.

The inaccurate diagnosis — that all socialist theories are based on — necessarily leads to inappropriate treatments and unworkable solutions. Abolishing private property and replacing it with social ownership does not solve the problem. It accomplishes only one thing: it transfers the control of the economy into the hands of political power.

It is nothing more than a power grab by the political elite.

Socialism does not work.

That is what's wrong with socialism.

A word of caution. The realization that faulty human nature is the cause of most social problems is not new. In fact, ancient philosophers and religions had recognized this problem. Christianity, among others, tried for centuries to 'cure' human nature and eliminate a wide variety of 'sins'. Most of these efforts failed and none of them had lasting effects except for the misery they caused. Why is that?

Religious institutions can and often did have very positive effects on religious communities. Their spiritual and communal power can be very helpful to society, the current anti-religion crusades notwithstanding. Somewhere along the line, however, they almost always go wrong. The mistake is always the same: the acquisition of power — political power —- too much power.

When some people become professional religious leaders everything changes. When the Christian religion became the Catholic Church the followers of Jesus became the subjects of the Pope. The leaders of the movement became the rulers of their followers. They added their newly acquired political power to their spiritual, ideological power. Soon a self-serving elite was born. All sorts of horrors followed. This pattern is recognizable in most organized religions. It can also be seen in non-religious ideological movements, in Marxism, Nazism, Communism and Bolshevism.

Socialism is not the only wrong solution to social problems; it is merely the newest one. Another lesson is that political power should be kept separate from all other kinds of power, economic, spiritual, military, ideological, and so on.

We need to constantly remind ourselves: social engineering does not work.

10.2 — Conspiracy

All these arguments against Socialism, Communism and Bolshevism beg another question: *So what, if Socialism does not work?*

What if the people want Socialism anyway?

Don't the American people have the right to be wrong?

Don't the American people have the right — guaranteed by the Constitution — to adopt any form of government they want?

Don't other peoples have the same right?

The answer to all these questions is YES, they do have these rights.

Our arguments, however, are not with the people.

They have the right to choose whatever form of government they want to have, including Bolshevism, Nazism, Communism, any sort of dictatorship, monarchy or theocracy. All they need to do is to amend the Constitution following proper procedures. They can also call a Constitutional Convention and create an entirely new constitution. Or they can have a revolution.

Furthermore, our arguments are not with the minorities.

We are not against African Americans.

We are not against Latinos.

We are not against women.

We are not against homosexuals.

We are not against the working classes.

We are not against the middle classes.

We are not against the professional classes.

We are not against lawyers, doctors, teachers or professors.

We are not against bankers, journalists, comedians or unions.

We are against Bolshevism.

Our arguments are with the New Left.

We are accusing New Left activists of lying to the people to entice them to make the wrong decision.

We are accusing New Left activists of hiding their true intentions.

We are accusing New Left theorists of conspiracy.

We are accusing the New Left of Conspiracy to Defraud the United States.

We are accusing the New Left of betrayal, treachery and treason.

The New Left advocates Social Justice but its real aim is to destroy private property, economic power, capitalism and America.

The New Left advocates equality and human rights but its real aim is to grab political power. They have already managed to acquire a substantial amount of such power. They used it to weaken the American economy, to damage American society, to undermine American military power and to endanger the Republic. They have done the same in many other countries.

The New Left made alliances with enemies of the United States, foreign and domestic, in violation of the oaths many of its members have sworn to.

These are serious accusations.

These accusations are political in their nature. While some of these accusation may constitute crimes, if proven, our intention here is not to urge criminal prosecutions.

This is a political fight over crucial political issues. Criminal prosecutions of selected people would only distract from our primary cause. Communism cannot and should not be fought in the courts of law or in Congressional hearings. That is a lesson we should have learnt from the McCarthy hearings.

Yet, Leftism and Minority Bolshevism must be fought if the Republic is to survive.

It must be fought in the court of public opinion.

10.3 — What if They Win?

To answer that question we first need to define what would constitute a victory of the New Left.

A Leftist victory would mean complete political control over the economy, society, culture, ideology and international relations, essentially over all aspects of life.

Notably, the New Left no longer offers any attractive vision of the future. They are not building Communism anymore. They gave up on the *dictatorship of the proletariat* long ago. They are only offering government health care along with unspecified increases in future government benefits.

Each member group of the Minority Bolshevism alliance is also offered some particular promise. Latinos would get "comprehensive immigration reform", meaning amnesty for illegal aliens. Gays would get the mainstreaming of homosexuality. Environmentalists would get to penalize industry in order to reduce carbon dioxide in the atmosphere. African Americans and radical feminists would get more political power for their leadership. And so on…

Presently, the New Left is attempting to carry out the controlled demolition of the US economy. Controlled in the sense of rapid, sector-by-sector government bailout and takeover of the entire economy. At the same time Leftists would like to keep the European economies afloat, as they are already under effective government control.

What would the controlled demolition of the US economy look like? It would be very much like FDR's New Deal — making the recession/depression much worse than necessary, and then stage a government "rescue" operation. Managed effectively, the population would support total government control in such a situation. Capitalists and other rich people would have to submit to and fully co-operate with the government or they would be destroyed. Markets would be strangled. Products and services would not be sold but distributed instead. Prices, wages, exchange rates and capital movements would be controlled by government agencies. Taxes would rise significantly. The banking system would be nationalized. Selected enemies of the New Left would be tried and convicted of various crimes. Many others would be fired from their jobs, or their careers would be sidelined.

Minorities and other New Left allies would be rewarded. Their standard of living would increase relative to other groups, although not in absolute terms. Gun control would be instituted: all guns would have to be registered and eventually turned over to the government. Illegal aliens would receive amnesty. Religious institutions would be taxed and regulated. Hate speech laws would become universal. Media unfriendly to Leftist causes would be closed down and several of its prominent representatives tried, convicted and jailed or otherwise ruined.

Intellectuals and bureaucrats would be in charge of everything. The country would be run much the same way as many higher education institutions are run presently. Uniform opinions, speech codes, regimented thinking, political correctness, multiculturalism would be enforced along with detailed regulation of everything else, including what we eat, how much we exercise, what movies we watch and what we think of them.

How bad can it be? What would we actually lose?

Prosperity, freedom, tradition, religion, our culture, the Republic, America, most everything.

In many ways the New Left has already won. Leftists control the ideological battlefield. Most competing ideologies are presently in retreat for various reasons.

Minority Bolsheviks also control the culture, both 'high culture' and popular culture. They dominate the media. They rule over education. They command the social agenda. They are on the verge of conquering the entire health care system. The lawyers are in their pockets.

The economy is limping. Financial capital has self-destructed; it is on life support at the mercy of political power. The military is busy fighting foreign enemies, many of whom enjoy the implicit support of American and Western Leftists.

So, have they won? And if not — why not?

Not yet. Their victories — though significant — are not yet irreversible. That is the definition that really matters: victory must be irreversible. New Left theorists know this. They know they have not yet won. But they are patient. Very patient.

While it is hazardous to make predictions of the future, there are clearly visible trends and observable patterns of behavior. There are many serious obstacles to irreversible Leftist victory. To get there from here is not an easy task, not even for the best theorists. It has only been done once in history. The Soviet Revolution triumphed in the most devastated country of a war-ravaged continent, but only with the help of the enemy. Its victory turned out to be hollow and temporary. It was based on treason.

As we have seen, the New Left's primary target is the economy. Capitalist economy is seriously wounded for a variety of reasons, and it is in distress all over the world, even in China. In America large segments of the economy have been monopolized by professional and other interest groups allied with the New Left. The rest of the economy is under constant pressure by government regulation, financial uncertainty and excess capacity.

The collapse of the American economy is in the interest of the New Left. We can assume that they will do everything in their power to make this collapse a reality. Such a collapse could and would be blamed on criminal 'banksters', greedy capitalists and the "one percent". Such a collapse would inevitably bring about a complete government takeover of the economy.

On the other hand, the collapse of the European economies could prove counterproductive for the New Left. A European economic collapse would effectively end the European Union and almost inevitably cause a resurgence of nationalism. Nationalism (along with religion) is the main ideological enemy of the Left (both old and new). Therefore, the New Leftists would try to keep the European economies afloat.

The potential collapse of China is another wild-card with unforeseeable consequences. China is also out of the reach of the New Left. After the strange demise of the Soviet Union, Chinese leaders instinctively know not trust the Leftists of the West.

Similarly, the collapse of the global financial system could have major unpredictable consequences. The demolition of the economy could easily spin out of control.

As mentioned above, the controlled demolition of the US economy was attempted before by the FDR Administration. President Roosevelt was largely successful in destroying the free enterprise system. His actions were rehearsed during a 'dry run' by the progressive administration of Woodrow Wilson during World War I.

Under FDR the economy came under almost total government control. Yet, at the end these changes did not stick; they turned out to be reversible, even after two decades. Why?

The answer is World War II. President Roosevelt had to pick an enemy: he had to choose whether to fight against capitalism in America or against German Nazism and Japanese fascism overseas. He chose to fight Hitler and Tojo instead of the US Congress and the Supreme Court. To win those fights, however, he needed a strong economy and a strong military. So he let the US economy recover in order to win the war. In the process he helped a nearly destroyed Soviet Union with a wrecked economy to rise and become a superpower with nuclear weapons.

FDR midwifed the birth of a Communist superpower, Soviet Russia, soon to be followed by Maoist China. The world barely survived this fallacy.

It is entirely possible that the New Left will face similar choices. If they win and destroy American capitalism there will be nothing to prevent the rise of a new superpower. Whoever or whatever that power turns out to be we may not be as lucky fighting World War III as we were fighting the previous two.

Even if the New Left wins all the battles, at the end they may lose the war. There is no guarantee whatsoever, that concentrated political power will behave the way Leftists would like. A new Napoleon might just throw out all the ideological baggage upon becoming emperor. A weakened Western Civilization may fall victim to an emerging young and energetic barbarian empire. Leftist intellectuals would fare rather poorly under many possible scenarios.

10.4 — The Right Side of Issues

What can we — the *Right* — do to counter the ideological and political onslaught of Leftists, the propaganda assault of Minority Bolsheviks?

First, we need to figure out what the Right Side of the issues really are; what positions we should take on individual issues. This is not easy. We are way behind the Leftists in both strategic thinking and tactical planning. On many issues we don't have coherent ideas, we often don't understand the issues themselves, and even less the interests and objectives of the various forces involved. We are clueless about the concerns of the individual minorities that together make up *Minority Bolshevism*.

We are still the *Old Right* facing the *New Left*.

We mostly react, and only react to new challenges by repeating old arguments that became irrelevant long time ago. On the other hand, most of us don't clearly understand what the fight is about, what our strengths are, or even what our most important values are. We often fall into traps set by our enemies. As a result we end up arguing irrelevant or unpopular positions, chosen for us by professional Bolshevik strategists.

Still we shouldn't despair. Most of our opponents are even more clueless. They are members of misled and exploited minorities whose leadership sold out to the New

Left long ago. We have to expose such leaders and their strategies. We need to break up and dismantle these *Minority Monopolies*. We cannot do this from the outside. We have to make an honest effort to understand these groups and to figure out a solution to their problems. Remember, they are not our predestined and inevitable enemies. They are victims of historical injustices, many of those perpetrated on them by their own allies. Mostly, they are against us because they don't know any better. We need to know better, so we can show them the right side of their issues.

We are often fighting battles on the terms of our enemies. We accept Leftist definitions of the issues; we let the Left identify the parties involved in the struggle along with their interests. We often accept Leftist depictions of our own positions and our own interests. Why? Because we do not have a theoretical structure we can support and depend on. We are still defending the ruins of our positions that were destroyed by the Leftists long ago.

We are accepting challenges and fights we should avoid, and engage in battles that are hopeless. We are not attacking the weak points of the Leftists because we don't bother to figure out what those might be.

We compromise when we should fight and fight when we should compromise.

We elect our leaders in a haphazard way, and select our goals arbitrarily and often randomly. We are disorganized.

We need to learn from our enemies.

What to do?

We need to organize the Right. We need to figure out who we are and who our friends are. We cannot just wait and hope that people will know what the right thing is to do. They don't know.

We need a new strategy. Not just a campaign strategy, designed for the next election, only to be immediately abandoned and forgotten. We need a long-term strategy, complete with philosophy and ideology. We need a marketing strategy, a coherent propaganda effort explaining our positions to the public. We need a new narrative.

We also need an action plan. We need to expose the Leftist plot, the Minority Bolshevik conspiracy. We need to expose its members, its structure, its funding, its history. We need to untangle the laws instituted to support Leftist positions and privileges.

We need to carry out devastating and well planned assaults on political correctness and multiculturalism. We need to liberate our culture from Leftist dogmas. We need to challenge the validity of unproven assumptions.

We need to win.

We need a new theory.

Contacts

Book

www.MinorityBolshevism.com

Author

www.ZurielRedwood.com

The End